Chapter 1 – Introduction to

Operating Systems

In the Computer System (comprises of Hardware and software), Hardware can only understand machine code (in the form of 0 and 1) which doesn't make any sense to a naive user.
We need a system which can act as an intermediary and manage all the processes and resources present in the system.

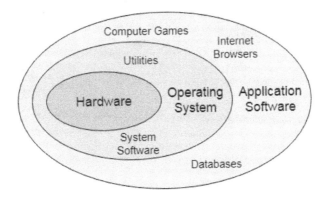

An **Operating System** can be defined as an **interface between user and hardware**. It is responsible for the execution of all the processes, Resource Allocation, CPU management, File Management and many other tasks.

The purpose of an operating system is to provide an environment in which a user can execute programs in convenient and efficient manner.

Structure of a Computer System

A Computer System consists of:

- Users (people who are using the computer)
- Application Programs (Compilers, Databases, Games, Video player, Browsers, etc.)
- System Programs (Shells, Editors, Compilers, etc.)
- Operating System (A special program which acts as an interface between user and hardware)
- Hardware (CPU, Disks, Memory, etc.)

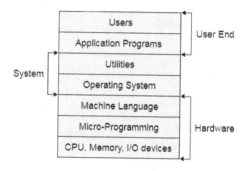

What does an Operating system do?

1. Process Management
2. Process Synchronization
3. Memory Management
4. CPU Scheduling
5. File Management
6. Security

Types of OS

There are many types of operating system exists in the current scenario:

Batch Operating System

In the era of 1970s, the Batch processing was very popular. The Jobs were executed in batches. People were used to have a single computer which was called mainframe.

In Batch operating system, access is given to more than one person; they submit their respective jobs to the system for the execution. The system put all of the jobs in a queue on the basis of first come first serve and then executes the jobs one by one. The users collect their respective output when all the jobs get executed.

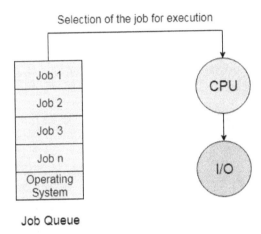

Job Queue

Disadvantages of Batch OS

Starvation
Batch processing suffers from starvation. If there are five jobs J1, J2, J3, J4, J4 and J5 present in the batch. If the execution time of J1 is very high then other four jobs will never be going to get executed or they will have to wait for a very high time. Hence the other processes get starved.

Not Interactive
Batch Processing is not suitable for the jobs which are dependent on the user's input. If a job requires the input of two numbers from the console then it will never be going to get it in the batch

processing scenario since the user is not present at the time of execution.

Multiprogramming Operating System

Multiprogramming is an extension to the batch processing where the CPU is kept always busy. Each process needs two types of system time: CPU time and IO time.
In multiprogramming environment, for the time a process does its I/O, The CPU can start the execution of other processes. Therefore, multiprogramming improves the efficiency of the system.

Multiprocessing Operating System

In Multiprocessing, Parallel computing is achieved. There are more than one processors present in the system which can execute more than one process at the same time. This will increase the throughput of the system.

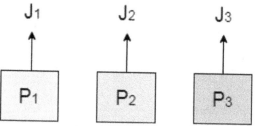

Real Time Operating System

In Real Time systems, each job carries a certain deadline within which the Job is supposed to be completed, otherwise the huge loss will be there or even if the result is produced then it will be completely useless.

The Application of a Real Time system exists in the case of military applications, if you want to drop a missile then the missile is supposed to be dropped with certain precision.

Chapter 2 – Process

Management

A Program does nothing unless its instructions are executed by a CPU. A program in execution is called a process. In order to accomplish its task, process needs the computer resources.
There may exist more than one process in the system which may require the same resource at the same time. Therefore, the operating system has to manage all the processes and the resources in a convenient and efficient way.

Some resources may need to be executed by one process at one time to maintain the consistency otherwise the system can become inconsistent and deadlock may occur.
The operating system is responsible for the following activities in connection with Process Management

1. Scheduling processes and threads on the CPUs.
2. Creating and deleting both user and system processes.
3. Suspending and resuming processes.
4. Providing mechanisms for process synchronization.
5. Providing mechanisms for process communication.

Process Attributes

The Attributes of the process are used by the Operating System to create the process control block (PCB) for each of them. This is also called context of the process. Attributes which are stored in the PCB are described below.

Process ID
When a process is created, a unique id is assigned to the process which is used for unique identification of the process in the system.

Program counter

A program counter stores the address of the last instruction of the process on which the process was suspended. The CPU uses this address when the execution of this process is resumed.

Process State

The Process, from its creation to the completion, goes through various states which are new, ready, running and waiting. We will discuss about them later in detail.

Priority

Every process has its own priority. The process with the highest priority among the processes gets the CPU first. This is also stored on the process control block.

General Purpose Registers

Every process has its own set of registers which are used to hold the data which is generated during the execution of the process.

List of open files

During the Execution, Every process uses some files which need to be present in the main memory. OS also maintains a list of open files in the PCB.

List of open devices

OS also maintain the list of all open devices which are used during the execution of the process.

Process States

State Diagram

The process, from its creation to completion, passes through various states. The minimum number of states is five.

The names of the states are not standardized although the process may be in one of the following states during execution.

New

A program which is going to be picked up by the OS into the main memory is called a new process.

Ready

Whenever a process is created, it directly enters in the ready state, in which, it waits for the CPU to be assigned. The OS picks the new processes from the secondary memory and put all of them in the main memory.

The processes which are ready for the execution and reside in the main memory are called ready state processes. There can be many processes present in the ready state.

Running

One of the processes from the ready state will be chosen by the OS depending upon the scheduling algorithm. Hence, if we have only one CPU in our system, the number of running processes for a particular time will always be one. If we have n processors in the system then we can have n processes running simultaneously.

Block or wait

From the Running state, a process can make the transition to the block or wait state depending upon the scheduling algorithm or the intrinsic behavior of the process.

When a process waits for a certain resource to be assigned or for the input from the user then the OS move this process to the block or wait state and assigns the CPU to the other processes.

Completion or termination

When a process finishes its execution, it comes in the termination state. All the context of the process (Process Control Block) will also be deleted the process will be terminated by the Operating system.

Suspend ready

A process in the ready state, which is moved to secondary memory from the main memory due to lack of the resources (mainly primary memory) is called in the **suspend ready** state.

If the main memory is full and a higher priority process comes for the execution then the OS have to make the room for the process in the main memory by throwing the lower priority process out into the secondary memory. The suspend ready processes remain in the secondary memory until the main memory gets available.

Suspend wait

Instead of removing the process from the ready queue, it's better to remove the blocked process which is waiting for some resources in the main memory. Since it is already waiting for some resource to get available hence it is better if it waits in the secondary memory and make room for the higher priority process. These processes complete their execution once the main memory gets available and their wait is finished.

Process Operations

Creation

Once the process is created, it will be ready and come into the ready queue (main memory) and will be ready for the execution.

Scheduling

Out of the many processes present in the ready queue, the Operating system chooses one process and start executing it. Selecting the process which is to be executed next, is known as scheduling.

Execution

Once the process is scheduled for the execution, the processor starts executing it. Process may come to the blocked or wait state during the execution then in that case the processor starts executing the other processes.

Deletion/killing

Once the purpose of the process gets over then the OS will kill the process. The Context of the process (PCB) will be deleted and the process gets terminated by the Operating system.

Process Schedulers

Operating system uses various schedulers for the process scheduling described below.

Long term scheduler

Long term scheduler is also known as job scheduler. It chooses the processes from the pool (secondary memory) and keeps them in the ready queue maintained in the primary memory.

Long Term scheduler mainly controls the degree of Multiprogramming. The purpose of long term scheduler is to choose a perfect mix of IO bound and CPU bound processes among the jobs present in the pool.

If the job scheduler chooses more IO bound processes then all of the jobs may reside in the blocked state all the time and the CPU will remain idle most of the time. This will reduce the degree of Multiprogramming. Therefore, the Job of long term scheduler is very critical and may affect the system for a very long time.

Short term scheduler

Short term scheduler is also known as CPU scheduler. It selects one of the Jobs from the ready queue and dispatch to the CPU for the execution.

A scheduling algorithm is used to select which job is going to be dispatched for the execution. The Job of the short term scheduler can be very critical in the sense that if it selects job whose CPU burst time is very high then all the jobs after that, will have to wait in the ready queue for a very long time.
This problem is called starvation which may arise if the short term scheduler makes some mistakes while selecting the job.

Medium term scheduler

Medium term scheduler takes care of the swapped out processes. If the running state processes needs some IO time for the completion then there is a need to change its state from running to waiting.

Medium term scheduler is used for this purpose. It removes the process from the running state to make room for the other processes. Such processes are the swapped out processes and this procedure is called swapping. The medium term scheduler is responsible for suspending and resuming the processes.

It reduces the degree of multiprogramming. The swapping is necessary to have a perfect mix of processes in the ready queue.

Process Queues

The Operating system manages various types of queues for each of the process states. The PCB related to the process is also stored in the queue of the same state. If the Process is moved from one state to another state then its PCB is also unlinked from the corresponding queue and added to the other state queue in which the transition is made.

There are the following queues maintained by the Operating system.

Job Queue
In starting, all the processes get stored in the job queue. It is maintained in the secondary memory. The long term scheduler (Job scheduler) picks some of the jobs and put them in the primary memory.

Ready Queue
Ready queue is maintained in primary memory. The short term scheduler picks the job from the ready queue and dispatch to the CPU for the execution.

Waiting Queue
When the process needs some IO operation in order to complete its execution, OS changes the state of the process from running to waiting. The context (PCB) associated with the process gets stored on the waiting queue which will be used by the Processor when the process finishes the IO.

Process Times

Arrival Time
The time at which the process enters into the ready queue is called the arrival time.

Burst Time
The total amount of time required by the CPU to execute the whole process is called the Burst Time. This does not include the waiting time. It is confusing to calculate the execution time for a process even before executing it hence the scheduling problems based on the burst time cannot be implemented in reality.

Completion Time
The Time at which the process enters into the completion state or the time at which the process completes its execution, is called completion time.

Turnaround time
The total amount of time spent by the process from its arrival to its completion, is called Turnaround time.

Waiting Time
The Total amount of time for which the process waits for the CPU to be assigned is called waiting time.

Response Time
The difference between the arrival time and the time at which the process first gets the CPU is called Response Time.

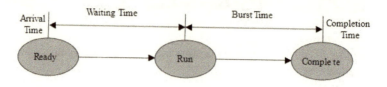

$$CT - AT = WT + BT$$

$$TAT = CT - AT$$

$$\text{Waiting Time} = TAT - BT$$

TAT ⟶ Turn around time

BT ⟶ Burst time

AT ⟶ Arrival time

Chapter 3 - Scheduling

In the uniprogrammming systems like MS DOS, when a process waits for any I/O operation to be done, the CPU remains idol. This is an overhead since it wastes the time and causes the problem of starvation. However, In Multiprogramming systems, the CPU doesn't remain idle during the waiting time of the Process and it starts executing other processes. Operating System has to define which process the CPU will be given.

In multiprogramming systems, the Operating system schedules the processes on the CPU to have the maximum utilization of it and this procedure is called CPU scheduling. The Operating System uses various scheduling algorithm to schedule the processes.
This is a task of the short term scheduler to schedule the CPU for the number of processes present in the Job Pool. Whenever the running process requests some IO operation then the short term scheduler saves the current context of the process (also called PCB) and changes its state from running to waiting. During the time, process is in waiting state; the Short term scheduler picks another process from the ready queue and assigns the CPU to this process. This procedure is called context switching.

What is saved in the Process Control Block?

The Operating system maintains a process control block during the lifetime of the process. The Process control block is deleted when the process is terminated or killed. There is the following information which is saved in the process control block and is changing with the state of the process.

Process ID
Process State
Pointer
Priority
Program Counter
CPU Registers
I/O Information
Accounting Information
etc.

Why do we need Scheduling?

In Multiprogramming, if the long term scheduler picks more I/O bound processes then most of the time, the CPU remains idol. The task of Operating system is to optimize the utilization of resources.

If most of the running processes change their state from running to waiting then there may always be a possibility of deadlock in the system. Hence to reduce this overhead, the OS needs to schedule the jobs to get the optimal utilization of CPU and to avoid the possibility to deadlock.

Scheduling Algorithms

There are various algorithms which are used by the Operating System to schedule the processes on the processor in an efficient way.

The Purpose of a Scheduling algorithm

1. Maximum CPU utilization
2. Fare allocation of CPU
3. Maximum throughput
4. Minimum turnaround time
5. Minimum waiting time
6. Minimum response time

There are the following algorithms which can be used to schedule the jobs.

First Come First Serve

It is the simplest algorithm to implement. The process with the minimal arrival time will get the CPU first. The lesser the arrival time, the sooner will the process gets the CPU. It is the non-preemptive type of scheduling.

Round Robin

In the Round Robin scheduling algorithm, the OS defines a time quantum (slice). All the processes will get executed in the cyclic way. Each of the process will get the CPU for a small amount of time (called time quantum) and then get back to the ready queue to wait for its next turn. It is a preemptive type of scheduling.

Shortest Job First

The job with the shortest burst time will get the CPU first. The lesser the burst time, the sooner will the process get the CPU. It is the non-preemptive type of scheduling.

Shortest remaining time first

It is the preemptive form of SJF. In this algorithm, the OS schedules the Job according to the remaining time of the execution.

Priority based scheduling

In this algorithm, the priority will be assigned to each of the processes. The higher the priority, the sooner will the process get the CPU. If the priority of the two processes is same then they will be scheduled according to their arrival time.

Highest Response Ratio Next

In this scheduling Algorithm, the process with highest response ratio will be scheduled next. This reduces the starvation in the system.

First Come First Served (FCFS)

First come first served (FCFS) scheduling algorithm simply schedules the jobs according to their arrival time. The job which comes first in the ready queue will get the CPU first. The lesser the arrival time of the job, the sooner will the job get the CPU. FCFS scheduling may cause the problem of starvation if the burst time of the first process is the longest among all the jobs.

Advantages of FCFS

- Simple
- Easy
- The early process in the queue is dealt with first

Disadvantages of FCFS

- The scheduling method is non preemptive, the process will run to the completion.
- Due to the non-preemptive nature of the algorithm, the problem of starvation may occur.
- Although it is easy to implement, but it is poor in performance since the average waiting time is higher as compare to other scheduling algorithms.

Example

Let's take an example of The FCFS scheduling algorithm. In the Following schedule, there are 5 processes with process ID P_0, P_1, P_2, P_3 and P_4. P_0 arrives at time 0, P_1 at time 1, P_2 at time 2, P_3 arrives at time 3 and Process P_4 arrives at time 4 in the ready queue. The processes and their respective Arrival and Burst time are given in the following table.

The Turnaround time and the waiting time are calculated by using the following formula.

$$\text{Turn Around Time} = \text{Completion Time} - \text{Arrival Time}$$
$$\text{Waiting Time} = \text{Turnaround time} - \text{Burst Time}$$

The average waiting Time is determined by summing the respective waiting time of all the processes and divided the sum by the total number of processes.

Process ID	Arrival Time	Burst Time	Completion Time	Turn Around Time	Waiting Time
0	0	2	2	2	0
1	1	6	8	7	1
2	2	4	12	8	4
3	3	9	21	18	9
4	4	12	33	29	17

P0	P1	P2	P3	P4	
0	2	8	12	21	33

Average Waiting Time=31/5

Convoy Effect in FCFS

FCFS may suffer from the convoy effect if the burst time of the first job is the highest among all. As in the real life, if a convoy is passing through the road then the other persons may get blocked until it passes completely. This can be simulated in the Operating System also.

If the CPU gets the processes of the higher burst time at the front end of the ready queue then the processes of lower burst time may get blocked which means they may never get the CPU if the job in the execution has a very high burst time. This is called convoy effect or starvation.

Example

In the Example, We have 3 processes named as P1, P2 and P3. The Burt Time of process P1 is highest.
The Turnaround time and the waiting time in the following table, are calculated by the formula,

Turn Around Time = Completion Time - Arrival Time
Waiting Time = Turn Around Time - Burst Time

In the First scenario, The Process P1 arrives at the first in the queue although; the burst time of the process is the highest among all. Since, the Scheduling algorithm, we are following is FCFS hence the CPU will execute the Process P1 first.

In this schedule, the average waiting time of the system will be very high. That is because of the convoy effect. The other processes P2, P3 have to wait for their turn for 40 units of time although their burst time is very low. This schedule suffers from starvation.

Process ID	Arrival Time	Burst Time	Completion Time	Turn Around Time	Waiting Time
1	0	40	40	40	0
2	1	3	43	42	39
3	1	1	44	43	42

P1	P2	P3	
0	40	43	44

Average Waiting Time = 81/3

In the Second scenario, If Process P1 would have arrived at the last of the queue and the other processes P2 and P3 at earlier then the problem of starvation would not be there.

Following example shows the deviation in the waiting times of both the scenarios. Although the length of the schedule is same that is 44 units but the waiting time will be lesser in this schedule.

Process ID	Arrival Time	Burst Time	Completion Time	Turn Around Time	Waiting Time
1	1	40	44	43	3
2	0	3	3	3	0
3	0	1	4	4	3

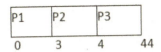

P1	P2	P3	
0	3	4	44

Average Waiting Time =6/3

FCFS with Overhead
In the above Examples, we are assuming that all the processes are the CPU bound processes only. We were also neglecting the context switching time.

However if the time taken by the scheduler in context switching is considered then the average waiting time of the system will be increased which also affects the efficiency of the system.
Context Switching is always an overhead. The Following Example described shows the efficiency will be affected if the context switching time is considered in the system.

Example
In the following Example, we are considering five processes P1, P2, P3, P4, P5 and P6. Their arrival time and Burst time are given below.

Process ID	Arrival Time	Burst Time
1	0	3
2	1	2
3	2	1
4	3	4
5	4	5
6	5	2

If the context switching time of the system is 1 unit then the Gantt chart of the system will be prepared as follows.

Given δ=1 unit;

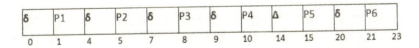

δ	P1	δ	P2	δ	P3	δ	P4	Δ	P5	δ	P6	
0	1	4	5	7	8	9	10	14	15	20	21	23

The system will take extra 1 unit of time (overhead) after the execution of every process to schedule the next process.

$$\text{Inefficiency} = (6/23) \times 100\%$$
$$\text{Efficiency } \eta = (1 - 6/23) \times 100\%$$

Shortest Job First (SJF)

Till now, we were scheduling the processes according to their arrival time (in FCFS scheduling). However, SJF scheduling algorithm, schedules the processes according to their burst time.

In SJF scheduling, the process with the lowest burst time, among the list of available processes in the ready queue, is going to be scheduled next.

However, it is very difficult to predict the burst time needed for a process hence this algorithm is very difficult to implement in the system.

Advantages of SJF

- Maximum throughput
- Minimum average waiting and turnaround time

Disadvantages of SJF

- May suffer with the problem of starvation
- It is not implementable because the exact Burst time for a process can't be known in advance.

There are different techniques available by which, the CPU burst time of the process can be determined. We will discuss them later in detail.

Example

In the following example, there are five jobs named as P1, P2, P3, P4 and P5. Their arrival time and burst time are given in the table below.

PID	Arrival Time	Burst Time	Completion Time	Turn Around Time	Waiting Time
1	1	7	8	7	0
2	3	3	13	10	7
3	6	2	10	4	2
4	7	10	31	24	14
5	9	8	21	12	4

Since, No Process arrives at time 0 hence; there will be an empty slot in the Gantt chart from time 0 to 1 (the time at which the first process arrives).

According to the algorithm, the OS schedules the process which is having the lowest burst time among the available processes in the ready queue.

Till now, we have only one process in the ready queue hence the scheduler will schedule this to the processor no matter what is its burst time.

This will be executed till 8 units of time. Till then we have three more processes arrived in the ready queue hence the scheduler will choose the process with the lowest burst time.

Among the processes given in the table, P3 will be executed next since it is having the lowest burst time among all the available processes.

So that's how the procedure will go on in Shortest Job First (SJF) scheduling algorithm.

	P1	P3	P2	P5	P4
0	1	8	10	13	21	31

Average Waiting Time = 27/5

Prediction of CPU Burst Time for a process in SJF
The SJF algorithm is one of the best scheduling algorithms since it provides the maximum throughput and minimal waiting time but

the problem with the algorithm is, the CPU burst time can't be known in advance.

We can approximate the CPU burst time for a process. There are various techniques which can be used to assume the CPU Burst time for a process. Our Assumption needs to be accurate in order to utilize the algorithm optimally.

There are the following techniques used for the assumption of CPU burst time for a process.

1. Static Techniques
2. Dynamic Techniques

Static Techniques

Process Size

We can predict the Burst Time of the process from its size. If we have two processes T_OLD and T_New and the actual burst time of the old process is known as 20 secs and the size of the process is 20 KB. We know that the size of P_NEW **is** 21 KB. Then the probability of P_New having the similar burst time as 20 secs is maximum.

If, P_OLD → 20 KB
P_New → 21 KB
BT(P_OLD) → 20 Secs
Then,
BT(P_New) → 20 secs

Hence, in this technique, we actually predict the burst time of a new process according to the burst time of an old process of similar size as of new process.

Process Type

We can also predict the burst time of the process according to its type. A Process can be of various types defined as follows.

- OS Process

    A Process can be an Operating system process like schedulers, compilers, program managers and many more system processes. Their burst time is generally lower for example, 3 to 5 units of time.

- **User Process**

  The Processes initiated by the users are called user processes. There can be three types of processes as follows.

- **Interactive Process**

  The Interactive processes are the one which interact with the user time to time or Execution of which totally depends upon the User inputs for example various games are such processes. There burst time needs to be lower since they don't need CPU for a large amount of time, they mainly depend upon the user's interactivity with the process hence they are mainly IO bound processes.

- **Foreground process**

  Foreground processes are the processes which are used by the user to perform their needs such as MS office, Editors, utility software etc. These types of processes have a bit higher burst time since they are a perfect mix of CPU and IO bound processes.

- **Background process**

  Background processes supports the execution of other processes. They work in hidden mode. For example, key logger is the process which records the keys pressed by the user and activities of the user on the system. They are mainly CPU bound processes and needs CPU for a higher amount of time.

Dynamic Techniques

Simple Averaging

In simple averaging, there are given list of n processes P(i).......P(n). Let T(i) denotes the burst time of the process P(i). Let $\tau(n)$ denotes the predicted burst time of Pth process. Then according to the simple averaging, the predicted burst time of process n+1 will be calculated as,

$$\tau(n+1) = (1/n) \sum T(i)$$

Where, $0<=i<=n$ and $\sum T(i)$ is the summation of actual burst time of all the processes available till now.

Exponential Averaging or Aging

Let, T_n be the actual burst time of nth process. $\tau(n)$ be the predicted burst time for nth process then the CPU burst time for the next process (n+1) will be calculated as,

$$\tau(n+1) = \alpha. Tn + (1-\alpha) . \tau(n)$$

Where, α is the smoothing. Its value lies between 0 and 1.

Shortest Remaining Time First (SRTF)

This Algorithm is the preemptive version of SJF scheduling. In SRTF, the execution of the process can be stopped after certain amount of time. At the arrival of every process, the short term scheduler schedules the process with the least remaining burst time among the list of available processes and the running process.

Once all the processes are available in the ready queue, No preemption will be done and the algorithm will work as SJF scheduling. The context of the process is saved in the Process Control Block when the process is removed from the execution and the next process is scheduled. This PCB is accessed on the next execution of this process.

Example

In this Example, there are five jobs P1, P2, P3, P4, P5 and P6. Their arrival time and burst time are given below in the table.

Process ID	Arrival Time	Burst Time	Completion Time	Turn Around Time	Waiting Time	Response Time
1	0	8	20	20	12	0
2	1	4	10	9	5	1
3	2	2	4	2	0	2
4	3	1	5	2	1	4
5	4	3	13	9	6	10
6	5	2	7	2	0	5

Average Waiting Time = 24/6

The Gantt chart is prepared according to the arrival and burst time given in the table.

- Since, at time 0, the only available process is P1 with CPU burst time 8. This is the only available process in the list therefore it is scheduled.
- The next process arrives at time unit 1. Since the algorithm we are using is SRTF which is a preemptive one, the current execution is stopped and the scheduler checks for the process with the least burst time. Till now, there are two processes available in the ready queue. The OS has executed P1 for one unit of time till now; the remaining burst time of P1 is 7 units. The burst time of Process P2 is 4 units. Hence Process P2 is scheduled on the CPU according to the algorithm.
- The next process P3 arrives at time unit 2. At this time, the execution of process P3 is stopped and the process with the least remaining burst time is searched. Since the process P3 has 2 unit of burst time hence it will be given priority over others.
- The Next Process P4 arrives at time unit 3. At this arrival, the scheduler will stop the execution of P4 and check which process is having least burst time among the available processes (P1, P2, P3 and P4). P1 and P2 are having the remaining burst time 7 units and 3 units respectively.
  P3 and P4 are having the remaining burst time 1 unit each. Since, both are equal hence the scheduling will be done according to their arrival time. P3 arrives earlier than P4 and therefore it will be scheduled again.
- The Next Process P5 arrives at time unit 4. Till this time, the Process P3 has completed its execution and it is no more in the list. The scheduler will compare the remaining burst

time of all the available processes. Since the burst time of process P4 is 1 which is least among all hence this will be scheduled.

- The Next Process P6 arrives at time unit 5, till this time, the Process P4 has completed its execution. We have 4 available processes till now, that are P1 (7), P2 (3), P5 (3) and P6 (2). The Burst time of P6 is the least among all hence P6 is scheduled. Since, now, all the processes are available hence the algorithm will now work same as SJF. P6 will be executed till its completion and then the process with the least remaining time will be scheduled.

Once all the processes arrive, No preemption is done and the algorithm will work as SJF.

SRTF GATE 2011 Example

If we talk about scheduling algorithm from the GATE point of view, they generally ask simple numerical questions about finding the average waiting time and Turnaround Time. Let's discuss the question asked in GATE 2011 on SRTF.

Given the arrival time and burst time of 3 jobs in the table below. Calculate the Average waiting time of the system.

Process ID	Arrival Time	Burst Time	Completion Time	Turn Around Time	Waiting Time
1	0	9	13	13	4
2	1	4	5	4	0
3	2	9	22	20	11

There are three jobs P1, P2 and P3. P1 arrives at time unit 0; it will be scheduled first for the time until the next process arrives. P2 arrives at 1 unit of time. Its burst time is 4 units which is least among the jobs in the queue. Hence it will be scheduled next.

At time 2, P3 will arrive with burst time 9. Since remaining burst time of P2 is 3 units which are least among the available jobs. Hence the processor will continue its execution till its completion. Because all the jobs have been arrived so no preemption will be done now and all the jobs will be executed till the completion according to SJF.

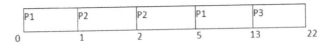

P1	P2	P2	P1	P3

0   1   2   5   13   22

Average Waiting Time = (4+0+11)/3 = 5 units

SRTF with Processes contains CPU and IO Time

Till now, we were considering the CPU bound jobs only. However, the process might need some IO operation or some resource to complete its execution. In this Example, we are considering, the IO bound processes.

In the Example, there are four jobs with process ID P1, P2, P3 and P4 are available. Their Arrival Time, and the CPU Burst time are given in the table below.

Process Id	Arrival Time	(Burst Time, IO Burst Time, Burst Time)
1	0	(3,2,2)
2	0	(1,3,1)
3	3	(3,1,2)
4	6	(5,4,5)

GANTT Chart Preparation

At time 0, the process P1 and P2 arrives. Since the algorithm we are using is SRTF hence, the process with the shortest burst time will be scheduled on the CPU. In this case, it is P2.

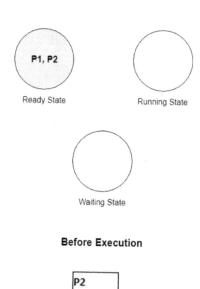

Before Execution

P2
0   1

From time 0 to time 1, P2 will be in running state.

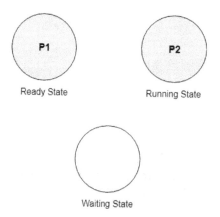

Time 0 to Time 1

P2 also needs some IO time in order to complete its execution. After 1 unit of execution, P2 will change its state from running to waiting. The processor becomes free to execute other jobs. Since No other process is available at this point of time other than P1 so P1 will get executed.

The following diagram illustrates the processes and states at Time 1. The process P2 went to waiting state and the CPU becomes idol at this time.

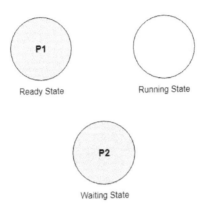

At Time 1

From time 1 to 3, since P2 is being in waiting state, and no other process is available in ready queue, hence the only available process P1 will be executed in this period of time.

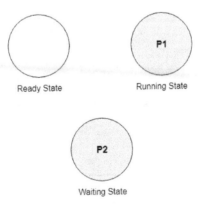

Time 1 to Time 3

At time 3, the process P3 arrived with the total CPU burst time of 5 units. Since the remaining burst time of P1 is lesser then P3 hence CPU will continue its execution.

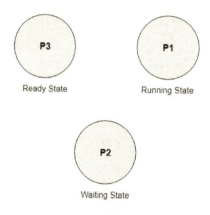

At Time 3

Hence, P1 will remain in the running state from time 3 to time 4.

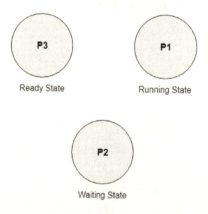

Time 3 to Time 4

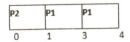

Since P1 is an IO bound process. At time unit 4, it will change its state from running to waiting. Processor becomes free for the execution of other jobs. Since P2 also becomes available at time 4 because it has completed the IO operation, it now needs another 1 unit of CPU burst time. P3 is also available and requires 5 units of total CPU burst time.

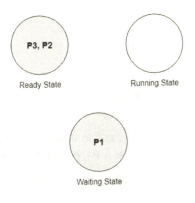

At Time 4

The process with the least remaining CPU burst time among the available processes will get executed. In our case, such process is P2 which requires 1 unit of burst time hence it will be given the CPU.

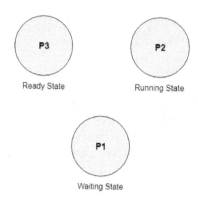

Ready State · Running State

Waiting State

Time 4 to Time 5

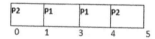

P2	P1		P1	P2	
0	1	3		4	5

At time 5, P2 is finished. P1 is still in waiting state. At this point of time, the only available process is P3, hence it will be given the CPU.

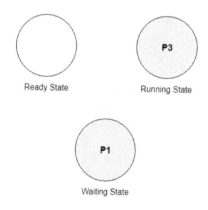

Ready State · Running State

Waiting State

At Time 5

From Time 5 to time 6, P3 will be in the running state; meanwhile, P1 will still be in waiting state.

Time 5 to Time 6

At Time 6

P2	P1	P1	P2	P3	
0	1	3	4	5	6

At time 6, the Process P4 arrives in the ready queue. The P1 has also done with the IO and becomes available for the execution. P3 is not yet finished and still needs another 2 unit of CPU burst time.

From time 6 to time 8, the reaming CPU burst time of Process P3 is least among the available processes, hence P3 will be given the CPU.

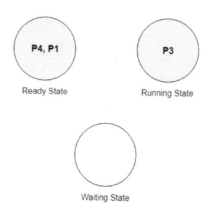

Ready State: P4, P1

Running State: P3

Waiting State

Time 6 to Time 8

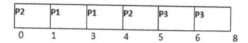

P2	P1	P1	P2	P3	P3

0   1   3   4   5   6   8

P3 needs some IO operation in order to complete its execution. At time 8, P3 will change its state from running to waiting. The CPU becomes free to execute the other processes. Process P4 and P1 are available out of which, the process with the least remaining burst time will get executed.

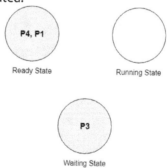

Ready State: P4, P1

Running State

Waiting State: P3

At Time 8

From time 8 to time 9, the process P1 will get executed.

Ready State — P4

Running State — P1

Waiting State — P3

Time 8 to Time 9

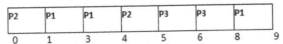

P2	P1	P1	P2	P3	P3	P1	
0	1	3	4	5	6	8	9

At time 9, the IO of process P3 is finished and it will now be available in the ready state along with P4 which is already waiting there for its turn. In order to complete its execution, it needs another 2 unit of burst time. P1 is in running state at this point of the time while no process is present in the waiting state.

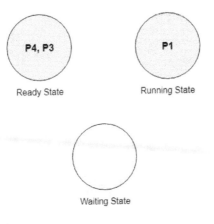

Ready State — P4, P3

Running State — P1

Waiting State

At Time 9

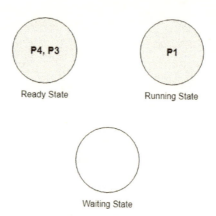

Ready State: P4, P3

Running State: P1

Waiting State

Time 9 to Time 10

From time 9 to 10 , the process P1 will get executed since its remaining CPU burst time is lesser then the processes P4 and P3 available in the ready queue.

P2	P1	P1	P2	P3	P3	P1	P1	

0   1   3   4   5   6   8   9   10

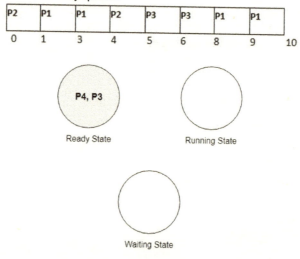

Ready State: P4, P3

Running State

Waiting State

At Time 10

At time 10, execution of P1 is finished, and now the CPU becomes idol. The process with the lesser CPU burst time among the ready processes will get the CPU turn.

From time 10 to 12, the process P3 will get executed till its completion because of the fact that its remaining CPU burst time is the between the two available processes. It needs 2 units of more CPU burst time, since No other process will be arrived in the ready state hence No preemption will be done and it will be executed till the completion.

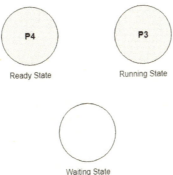

Time 10 to Time 12

P2	P1	P1	P2	P3	P3	P1	P1	P3	
0	1	3	4	5	6	8	9	10	12

At time 12, the process P3 will get completed, since there is only one process P4 available in the ready state hence P4 will be given the CPU.

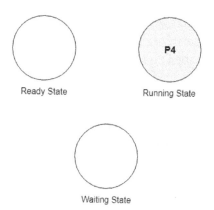

Ready State   Running State

Waiting State

Time 12 to Time 17

P4 needs 5 units of CPU burst time before IO, hence it will be executed till time 17 (for 5 units) and then it will change its state from running to waiting.

P2	P1	P1	P2	P3	P3	P1	P1	P3	P4
0	1	3	4	5	6	8	9	10	12	17

At time 17, the Process P4 changes its state from running to waiting. Since this is the only process in the system hence the CPU will remain idol until P4 becomes available again.

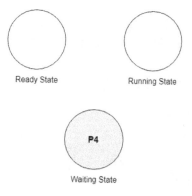

Ready State   Running State

P4

Waiting State

Time 17 to Time 21

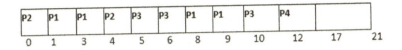

P2	P1	P1	P2	P3	P3	P1	P1	P3	P4	

0   1   3   4   5   6   8   9   10   12   17   21

At time 21, P4 will be done with the IO operation and becomes available in the ready state.

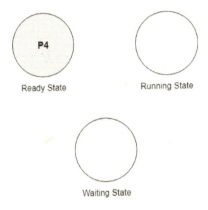

Ready State   Running State

Waiting State

At Time 21

From time 21, the process P4 will get scheduled. Since No other process is in ready queue hence the processor don't have any choice. It will be executed till completion.

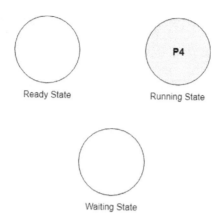

Ready State   Running State

Waiting State

Time 21 to Time 26

Final Gantt chart

P2	P1	P1	P2	P3	P3	P1	P1	P3	P4		P4

0   1   3   4   5   6   8   9   10   12   17   21   26

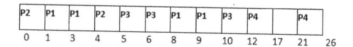

Process Id	Arrival Time	Total CPU Burst Time	Completion Time	Turn Around Time	Waiting Time
1	0	5	10	10	5
2	0	2	5	5	3
3	3	5	12	9	4
4	6	10	26	20	10

Average waiting Time = (5+3+4+10)/4 = 22/4 units

Round Robin

Round Robin scheduling algorithm is one of the most popular scheduling algorithm which can actually be implemented in most of the operating systems. This is the **preemptive version** of first come first serve scheduling. The Algorithm focuses on Time Sharing. In this algorithm, every process gets executed in a **cyclic way**. A certain time slice is defined in the system which is called time **quantum**.

Each process present in the ready queue is assigned the CPU for that time quantum, if the execution of the process is completed during that time then the process will **terminate** else the process will go back to the **ready queue** and waits for the next turn to complete the execution.

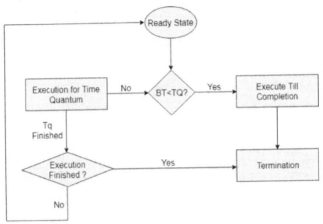

Advantages

- It can be actually implementable in the system because it is not depending on the burst time.
- It doesn't suffer from the problem of starvation or convoy effect.
- All the jobs get a fare allocation of CPU.

Disadvantages

- The higher the time quantum, the higher the response time in the system.
- The lower the time quantum, the higher the context switching overhead in the system.
- Deciding a perfect time quantum is really a very difficult task in the system.

Example

In the following example, there are six processes named as P1, P2, P3, P4, P5 and P6. Their arrival time and burst time are given below in the table. The time quantum of the system is 4 units.

Process ID	Arrival Time	Burst Time
1	0	5
2	1	6
3	2	3
4	3	1
5	4	5
6	6	4

According to the algorithm, we have to maintain the ready queue and the Gantt chart. The structure of both the data structures will be changed after every scheduling.

Ready Queue

Initially, at time 0, process P1 arrives which will be scheduled for the time slice 4 units. Hence in the ready queue, there will be only one process P1 at starting with CPU burst time 5 units.

GANTT chart

The P1 will be executed for 4 units first.

Ready Queue

Meanwhile the execution of P1, four more processes P2, P3, P4 and P5 arrives in the ready queue. P1 has not completed yet, it needs another 1 unit of time hence it will also be added back to the ready queue.

P2	P3	P4	P5	P1
6	3	1	5	1

GANTT chart

After P1, P2 will be executed for 4 units of time which is shown in the Gantt chart.

P1	P2	
0	4	8

Ready Queue

During the execution of P2, one more process P6 is arrived in the ready queue. Since P2 has not completed yet hence, P2 will also be added back to the ready queue with the remaining burst time 2 units.

P3	P4	P5	P1	P6	P2
3	1	5	1	4	2

GANTT chart

After P1 and P2, P3 will get executed for 3 units of time since its CPU burst time is only 3 seconds.

P1	P2	P3
0	4	8	11

Ready Queue

Since P3 has been completed, hence it will be terminated and not be added to the ready queue. The next process will be executed is P4.

P4	P5	P1	P6	P2
1	5	1	4	2

GANTT chart

After, P1, P2 and P3, P4 will get executed. Its burst time is only 1 unit which is lesser then the time quantum hence it will be completed.

P1	P2	P3	P4
0	4	8	11	12

Ready Queue

The next process in the ready queue is P5 with 5 units of burst time. Since P4 is completed hence it will not be added back to the queue.

GANTT chart

P5 will be executed for the whole time slice because it requires 5 units of burst time which is higher than the time slice.

P1	P2	P3	P4	P5	
0	4	8	11	12	16

Ready Queue

P5 has not been completed yet; it will be added back to the queue with the remaining burst time of 1 unit.

GANTT chart

The process P1 will be given the next turn to complete its execution. Since it only requires 1 unit of burst time hence it will be completed.

P1	P2	P3	P4	P5	P1	
0	4	8	11	12	16	17

Ready Queue

P1 is completed and will not be added back to the ready queue. The next process P6 requires only 4 units of burst time and it will be executed next.

GANTT chart

P6 will be executed for 4 units of time till completion.

P1	P2	P3	P4	P5	P1	P6
0	4	8	11	12	16	17	21

Ready Queue
Since P6 is completed, hence it will not be added again to the queue. There are only two processes present in the ready queue. The Next process P2 requires only 2 units of time.

GANTT chart
P2 will get executed again, since it only requires only 2 units of time hence this will be completed.

P1	P2	P3	P4	P5	P1	P6	P2
0	4	8	11	12	16	17	21	23

Ready Queue
Now, the only available process in the queue is P5 which requires 1 unit of burst time. Since the time slice is of 4 units hence it will be completed in the next burst.

GANTT chart
P5 will get executed till completion.

P1	P2	P3	P4	P5	P1	P6	P2	P5
0	4	8	11	12	16	17	21	23	24

The completion time, Turnaround time and waiting time will be calculated as shown in the table below.
As, we know,

Turn Around Time = Completion Time - Arrival Time

Waiting Time = Turn Around Time - Burst Time

Process ID	Arrival Time	Burst Time	Completion Time	Turn Around Time	Waiting Time
1	0	5	17	17	12
2	1	6	23	22	16
3	2	3	11	9	6
4	3	1	12	9	8
5	4	5	24	20	15
6	6	4	21	15	11

Average Waiting Time = (12+16+6+8+15+11)/6 = 76/6 units

Highest Response Ratio Next (HRRN)

Highest Response Ratio Next (HRNN) is one of the most optimal scheduling algorithms. This is a non-preemptive algorithm in which, the scheduling is done on the basis of an extra parameter called Response Ratio. A Response Ratio is calculated for each of the available jobs and the Job with the highest response ratio is given priority over the others.

Response Ratio is calculated by the given formula.
$$Response\ Ratio = (W+S)/S$$
Where,
W → Waiting Time
S → Service Time or Burst Time

If we look at the formula, we will notice that the job with the shorter burst time will be given priority but it is also including an extra factor called waiting time. Since,
HRNN α W
HRNN α (1/S)
Hence,

1. This algorithm not only favors shorter job but it also concern the waiting time of the longer jobs.

2. Its mode is non preemptive hence context switching is minimal in this algorithm.

HRNN Example
In the following example, there are 5 processes given. Their arrival time and Burst Time are given in the table.

Process ID	Arrival Time	Burst Time
0	0	3
1	2	5
2	4	4
3	6	1
4	8	2

At time 0, The Process P0 arrives with the CPU burst time of 3 units. Since it is the only process arrived till now hence this will get scheduled immediately.

P0 is executed for 3 units, meanwhile, only one process P1 arrives at time 3. This will get scheduled immediately since the OS doesn't have a choice.

P1 is executed for 5 units. Meanwhile, all the processes get available. We have to calculate the Response Ratio for all the remaining jobs.
RR (P2) = ((8-4) +4)/4 = 2
RR (P3) = (2+1)/1 = 3
RR (P4) = (0+2)/2 = 1

Since, the Response ratio of P3 is higher hence P3 will be scheduled first.

PO   P1   P3
0   3   8   9

P3 is scheduled for 1 unit. The next available processes are P2 and P4. Let's calculate their Response ratio.
RR (P2) = (5+4)/4 = 2.25
RR (P4) = (1+2)/2 = 1.5

The response ratio of P2 is higher hence P2 will be scheduled.

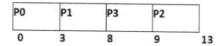

PO	P1	P3	P2
0	3	8	9	13

Now, the only available process is P4 with the burst time of 2 units, since there is no other process available hence this will be scheduled.

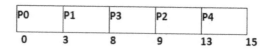

PO	P1	P3	P2	P4
0	3	8	9	13	15

Process ID	Arrival Time	Burst Time	Completion Time	Turn Around Time	Waiting Time
0	0	3	3	3	0
1	2	5	8	6	1
2	4	4	13	9	5
3	6	1	9	3	2
4	8	2	15	7	5

Average Waiting Time = 13/5

Priority

In Priority scheduling, there is a priority number assigned to each process. In some systems, the lower the number, the higher the priority. While, in the others, the higher the number, the higher will be the priority. The Process with the higher priority among the available processes is given the CPU. There are two types of priority scheduling algorithm exists. One is **Preemptive** priority scheduling while the other is **Non-Preemptive** Priority scheduling.

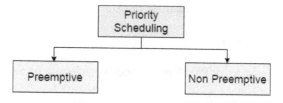

The priority number assigned to each of the process may or may not vary. If the priority number doesn't change itself throughout the process, it is called **static priority**, while if it keeps changing itself at the regular intervals, it is called **dynamic priority**.

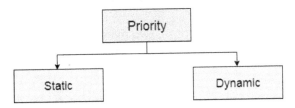

Non-Preemptive Priority

In the Non-Preemptive Priority scheduling, The Processes are scheduled according to the priority number assigned to them. Once the process gets scheduled, it will run till the completion. Generally, the lower the priority number, the higher is the priority of the process. The people might get confused with the priority numbers, hence in the GATE, there clearly mention which one is the highest priority and which one is the lowest one.

Example

In the Example, there are 7 processes P1, P2, P3, P4, P5, P6 and P7. Their priorities, Arrival Time and burst time are given in the table.

Process ID	Priority	Arrival Time	Burst Time
1	2	0	3
2	6	2	5
3	3	1	4
4	5	4	2
5	7	6	9
6	4	5˙	4
7	10	7	10

We can prepare the Gantt chart according to the Non Preemptive priority scheduling.

The Process P1 arrives at time 0 with the burst time of 3 units and the priority number 2. Since No other process has arrived till now hence the OS will schedule it immediately.

Meanwhile the execution of P1, two more Processes P2 and P3 are arrived. Since the priority of P3 is 3 hence the CPU will execute P3 over P2.

Meanwhile the execution of P3, All the processes get available in the ready queue. The Process with the lowest priority number will be given the priority. Since P6 has priority number assigned as 4 hence it will be executed just after P3.

After P6, P4 has the least priority number among the available processes; it will get executed for the whole burst time.

Since all the jobs are available in the ready queue hence All the Jobs will get executed according to their priorities. If two jobs have similar priority number assigned to them, the one with the least arrival time will be executed.

P1	P3	P6	P4	P2	P5	P7
0	3	7	11	13	18	27	37

From the GANTT Chart prepared, we can determine the completion time of every process. The turnaround time, waiting time and response time will be determined.

Turn Around Time = Completion Time - Arrival Time

Waiting Time = Turn Around Time - Burst Time

Process ID	Priority	Arrival Time	Burst Time	Completion Time	Turnaround Time	Waiting Time	Response Time
1	2	0	3	3	3	0	0
2	6	2	5	18	16	11	13
3	3	1	4	7	6	2	3
4	5	4	2	13	9	7	11
5	7	6	9	27	21	12	18
6	4	5	4	11	6	2	7
7	10	7	10	37	30	18	27

Average Waiting Time = (0+11+2+7+12+2+18)/7 = 52/7 units

Preemptive Priority

In Preemptive Priority Scheduling, at the time of arrival of a process in the ready queue, its Priority is compared with the priority of the other processes present in the ready queue as well as with the one which is being executed by the CPU at that point of time. The One with the highest priority among all the available processes will be given the CPU next.

The difference between preemptive priority scheduling and non-preemptive priority scheduling is that, in the preemptive priority scheduling, the job which is being executed can be stopped at the arrival of a higher priority job.

Once all the jobs get available in the ready queue, the algorithm will behave as non-preemptive priority scheduling, which means the job scheduled will run till the completion and no preemption will be done.

Example
There are 7 processes P1, P2, P3, P4, P5, P6 and P7 given. Their respective priorities, Arrival Times and Burst times are given in the table below.

Process ID	Priority	Arrival Time	Burst Time
1	2(L)	0	1
2	6	1	7
3	3	2	3
4	5	3	6
5	4	4	5
6	10(H)	5	15
7	9	15	8

GANTT Chart Preparation

At time 0, P1 arrives with the burst time of 1 units and priority 2. Since no other process is available hence this will be scheduled till next job arrives or its completion (whichever is lesser).

```
P1
0       1
```

At time 1, P2 arrives. P1 has completed its execution and no other process is available at this time hence the Operating system has to schedule it regardless of the priority assigned to it.

```
P1      P2
0       1       2
```

The Next process P3 arrives at time unit 2, the priority of P3 is higher to P2. Hence the execution of P2 will be stopped and P3 will be scheduled on the CPU.

```
P1      P2      P3
0       1       2         5
```

During the execution of P3, three more processes P4, P5 and P6 becomes available. Since, all these three have the priority lower to the process in execution so PS can't preempt the process. P3 will complete its execution and then P5 will be scheduled with the priority highest among the available processes.

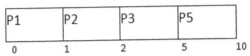

P1	P2	P3	P5	
0	1	2	5	10

Meanwhile the execution of P5, all the processes got available in the ready queue. At this point, the algorithm will start behaving as Non Preemptive Priority Scheduling. Hence now, once all the processes get available in the ready queue, the OS just took the process with the highest priority and execute that process till completion. In this case, P4 will be scheduled and will be executed till the completion.

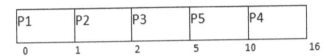

P1	P2	P3	P5	P4	
0	1	2	5	10	16

Since P4 is completed, the other process with the highest priority available in the ready queue is P2. Hence P2 will be scheduled next.

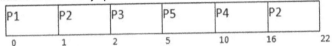

P1	P2	P3	P5	P4	P2	
0	1	2	5	10	16	22

P2 is given the CPU till the completion. Since its remaining burst time is 6 units hence P7 will be scheduled after this.

P1	P2	P3	P5	P4	P2	P7	
0	1	2	5	10	16	22	30

The only remaining process is P6 with the least priority, the Operating System has no choice unless of executing it. This will be executed at the last.

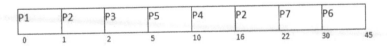

P1	P2	P3	P5	P4	P2	P7	P6	
0	1	2	5	10	16	22	30	45

The Completion Time of each process is determined with the help of GANTT chart. The turnaround time and the waiting time can be calculated by the following formula.

Turnaround Time = Completion Time - Arrival Time
Waiting Time = Turn Around Time - Burst Time

Process ID	Priority	Arrival Time	Burst Time	Completion Time	Turn-around Time	Waiting Time
1	2	0	1	1	1	0
2	6	1	7	22	21	14
3	3	2	3	5	3	0
4	5	3	6	16	13	7
5	4	4	5	10	6	1
6	10	5	15	45	40	25
7	9	6	8	30	24	16

Average Waiting Time = (0+14+0+7+1+25+16)/7 = 63/7 = 9 units

Chapter 4 - Synchronization

When two or more process cooperates with each other, their order of execution must be preserved otherwise there can be conflicts in their execution and inappropriate outputs can be produced.

A cooperative process is the one which can affect the execution of other process or can be affected by the execution of other process. Such processes need to be synchronized so that their order of execution can be guaranteed.

The procedure involved in preserving the appropriate order of execution of cooperative processes is known as Process Synchronization. There are various synchronization mechanisms that are used to synchronize the processes.

Race Condition
A Race Condition typically occurs when two or more threads try to read, write and possibly make the decisions based on the memory that they are accessing concurrently.

Critical Section
The regions of a program that try to access shared resources and may cause race conditions are called critical section. To avoid race condition among the processes, we need to assure that only one process at a time can execute within the critical section.

The Critical Section Problem

Critical Section is the part of a program which tries to access shared resources. That resource may be any resource in a computer like a memory location, Data structure, CPU or any IO device.

The critical section cannot be executed by more than one process at the same time; operating system faces the difficulties in allowing and disallowing the processes from entering the critical section.

The critical section problem is used to design a set of protocols which can ensure that the Race condition among the processes will never arise.

In order to synchronize the cooperative processes, our main task is to solve the critical section problem. We need to provide a solution in such a way that the following conditions can be satisfied.

Requirements of Synchronization mechanisms

Primary Requirements

1. Mutual Exclusion
Our solution must provide mutual exclusion. By Mutual Exclusion, we mean that if one process is executing inside critical section then the other process must not enter in the critical section.

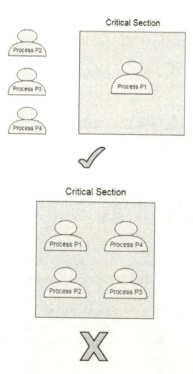

2. Progress

Progress means that if one process doesn't need to execute into critical section then it should not stop other processes to get into the critical section.

Secondary Requirements

1. Bounded Waiting

We should be able to predict the waiting time for every process to get into the critical section. The process must not be endlessly waiting for getting into the critical section.

2. Architectural Neutrality

Our mechanism must be architectural natural. It means that if our solution is working fine on one architecture then it should also run on the other ones as well.

Lock Variable

This is the simplest synchronization mechanism. This is a Software Mechanism implemented in User mode. This is a busy waiting solution which can be used for more than two processes.

In this mechanism, a Lock variable **lock** is used. Two values of lock can be possible, either 0 or 1. Lock value 0 means that the critical section is vacant while the lock value 1 means that it is occupied.

A process which wants to get into the critical section first checks the value of the lock variable. If it is 0 then it sets the value of lock as 1 and enters into the critical section, otherwise it waits.

The pseudo code of the mechanism looks like following.
Entry Section →
While (lock! = 0);
Lock = 1;
//Critical Section
Exit Section →
Lock =0;

If we look at the Pseudo Code, we find that there are three sections in the code. Entry Section, Critical Section and the exit section.

Initially the value of lock variable is 0. The process which needs to get into the critical section, enters into the entry section and checks the condition provided in the while loop.

The process will wait infinitely until the value of lock is 1 (that is implied by while loop). Since, at the very first time critical section is vacant hence the process will enter the critical section by setting the lock variable as 1.

When the process exits from the critical section, then in the exit section, it reassigns the value of lock as 0.

Every Synchronization mechanism is judged on the basis of four conditions.

1. Mutual Exclusion

2. Progress

3. Bounded Waiting

4. Portability

Out of the four parameters, Mutual Exclusion and Progress must be provided by any solution. Let's analyze this mechanism on the basis of the above mentioned conditions.

Mutual Exclusion

The lock variable mechanism doesn't provide Mutual Exclusion in some of the cases. This can be better described by looking at the pseudo code by the Operating System point of view I.E. Assembly code of the program. Let's convert the Code into the assembly language.

1. Load Lock, R0

2. CMP R0, #0

3. JNZ Step 1

4. Store #1, Lock

5. Store #0, Lock

Let us consider that we have two processes P1 and P2. The process P1 wants to execute its critical section. P1 gets into the entry section. Since the value of lock is 0 hence P1 changes its value from 0 to 1 and enters into the critical section.

Meanwhile, P1 is preempted by the CPU and P2 gets scheduled. Now there is no other process in the critical section and the value of lock variable is 0. P2 also wants to execute its critical section. It enters into the critical section by setting the lock variable to 1.

Now, CPU changes P1's state from waiting to running. P1 is yet to finish its critical section. P1 has already checked the value of lock variable and remembers that its value was 0 when it previously checked it. Hence, it also enters into the critical section without checking the updated value of lock variable.

Now, we got two processes in the critical section. According to the condition of mutual exclusion, more than one process in the critical section must not be present at the same time. Hence, the lock variable mechanism doesn't guarantee the mutual exclusion.

The problem with the lock variable mechanism is that, at the same time, more than one process can see the vacant tag and more than one process can enter in the critical section. Hence, the lock variable doesn't provide the mutual exclusion that's why it cannot be used in general.

Since, this method is failed at the basic step; hence, there is no need to talk about the other conditions to be fulfilled.

Test Set Lock Mechanism

Modification in the assembly code

In lock variable mechanism, Sometimes Process reads the old value of lock variable and enters the critical section. Due to this reason, more than one process might get into critical section. However, the code shown in the part one of the following section can be replaced with the code shown in the part two. This doesn't affect the algorithm but, by doing this, we can manage to provide the mutual exclusion to some extent but not completely.

In the updated version of code, the value of Lock is loaded into the local register Ro and then value of lock is set to 1.

However, in step 3, the previous value of lock (that is now stored into Ro) is compared with 0. if this is 0 then the process will simply enter into the critical section otherwise will wait by executing continuously in the loop.

The benefit of setting the lock immediately to 1 by the process itself is that, now the process which enters into the critical section carries the updated value of lock variable that is 1.

In the case when it gets preempted and scheduled again then also it will not enter the critical section regardless of the current value of the lock variable as it already knows what the updated value of lock variable is.

Section 1	Section 2
1. Load Lock, Ro	1. Load Lock, Ro
2. CMP Ro, #0	2. Store #1, Lock
3. JNZ step1	3. CMP Ro, #0
4. store #1, Lock	4. JNZ step 1

TSL Instruction

However, the solution provided in the above segment provides mutual exclusion to some extent but it doesn't make sure that the mutual exclusion will always be there. There is a possibility of having more than one process in the critical section.

What if the process gets preempted just after executing the first instruction of the assembly code written in section 2? In that case, it will carry the old value of lock variable with it and it will enter into the critical section regardless of knowing the current value of lock variable. This may make the two processes present in the critical section at the same time.

To get rid of this problem, we have to make sure that the preemption must not take place just after loading the previous value of lock variable and before setting it to 1. The problem can be solved if we can be able to merge the first two instructions.

In order to address the problem, the operating system provides a special instruction called Test Set Lock (TSL) instruction which simply loads the value of lock variable into the local register Ro and sets it to 1 simultaneously.

The process which executes the TSL first will enter into the critical section and no other process after that can enter until the first process comes out. No process can execute the critical section even in the case of preemption of the first process.
The assembly code of the solution will look like following.

1. TSL Lock, Ro

2. CMP Ro, #0

3. JNZ step 1

Let's examine TSL on the basis of the four conditions.

Mutual Exclusion
Mutual Exclusion is guaranteed in TSL mechanism since a process can never be preempted just before setting the lock variable. Only one process can see the lock variable as 0 at a particular time and that's why, the mutual exclusion is guaranteed.

Progress
According to the definition of the progress, a process which doesn't want to enter in the critical section should not stop other processes to get into it. In TSL mechanism, a process will execute the TSL instruction only when it wants to get into the critical section. The value of the lock will always be 0 if no process doesn't want to enter into the critical section hence the progress is always guaranteed in TSL.

Bounded Waiting

Bounded Waiting is not guaranteed in TSL. Some process might not get a chance for so long. We cannot predict for a process that it will definitely get a chance to enter in critical section after a certain time.

Architectural Neutrality

TSL doesn't provide Architectural Neutrality. It depends on the hardware platform. The TSL instruction is provided by the operating system. Some platforms might not provide that. Hence it is not Architectural natural.

Priority Inversion

In TSL mechanism, there can be a problem of priority inversion. Let's say that there are two cooperative processes, P1 and P2.

The priority of P1 is 2 while that of P2 is 1. P1 arrives earlier and got scheduled by the CPU. Since it is a cooperative process and wants to execute in the critical section hence it will enter in the critical section by setting the lock variable to 1.

Now, P2 arrives in the ready queue. The priority of P2 is higher than P1 hence according to priority scheduling, P2 is scheduled and P1 got preempted. P2 is also a cooperative process and wants to execute inside the critical section.

Although, P1 got preempted but it the value of lock variable will be shown as 1 since P1 is not completed and it is yet to finish its critical section.

P1 needs to finish the critical section but according to the scheduling algorithm, CPU is with P2. P2 wants to execute in the critical section, but according to the synchronization mechanism, critical section is with P1.

This is a kind of lock where each of the process neither executes nor completes. Such kind of lock is called Spin Lock.

This is different from deadlock since they are not in blocked state. One is in ready state and the other is in running state, but neither of the two is being executed.

Turn Variable or Strict Alternation Approach

Turn Variable or Strict Alternation Approach is the software mechanism implemented at user mode. It is a busy waiting solution which can be implemented only for two processes. In this approach, A turn variable is used which is actually a lock.

This approach can only be used for only two processes. In general, let the two processes be Pi and Pj. They share a variable called turn variable. The pseudo code of the program can be given as following.

For Process Pi
Non - CS
while (turn ! = i);
Critical Section
turn = j;
Non - CS

For Process Pj
Non - CS
while (turn ! = j);
Critical Section
turn = i ;
Non - CS

The actual problem of the lock variable approach was the fact that the process was entering in the critical section only when the lock variable is 1. More than one process could see the lock variable as 1 at the same time hence the mutual exclusion was not guaranteed there.

This problem is addressed in the turn variable approach. Now, A process can enter in the critical section only in the case when the value of the turn variable equal to the PID of the process.

There are only two values possible for turn variable, i or j. if its value is not i then it will definitely be j or vice versa.

In the entry section, in general, the process Pi will not enter in the critical section until its value is j or the process Pj will not enter in the critical section until its value is i.

Initially, two processes Pi and Pj are available and want to execute into critical section.

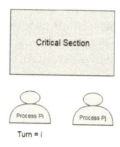

The turn variable is equal to i hence Pi will get the chance to enter into the critical section. The value of Pi remains I until Pi finishes critical section.

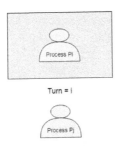

Turn = i

Pi finishes its critical section and assigns j to turn variable. Pj will get the chance to enter into the critical section. The value of turn remains j until Pj finishes its critical section.

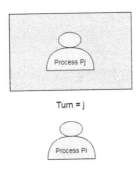

Turn = j

Analysis of Strict Alternation approach

Let's analyze Strict Alternation approach on the basis of four requirements.

Mutual Exclusion

The strict alternation approach provides mutual exclusion in every case. This procedure works only for two processes. The pseudo code is different for both of the processes. The process will only enter when it sees that the turn variable is equal to its Process ID otherwise not Hence No process can enter in the critical section regardless of its turn.

Progress

Progress is not guaranteed in this mechanism. If Pi doesn't want to get enter into the critical section on its turn then Pj got blocked for infinite time. Pj has to wait for so long for its turn since the turn variable will remain o until Pi assigns it to j.

Portability

The solution provides portability. It is a pure software mechanism implemented at user mode and doesn't need any special instruction from the Operating System.

Mutual Exclusion	✓
Progress	✗
Bounded Waiting	✓
Portability	✓

Interested Variable Mechanism

We have to make sure that the progress must be provided by our synchronization mechanism. In the turn variable mechanism, progress was not provided due to the fact that the process which doesn't want to enter in the critical section does not consider the other interested process as well.

The other process will also have to wait regardless of the fact that there is no one inside the critical section. If the operating system can make use of an extra variable along with the turn variable then this problem can be solved and our problem can provide progress to most of the extent.

Interested variable mechanism makes use of an extra Boolean variable to make sure that the progress is provided.

For Process Pi
Non CS
Int[i] = T ;
while (Int[j] == T);
Critical Section
Int[i] = F ;

For Process Pj
Non CS
Int [1] = T ;
while (Int[i] == T) ;
Critical Section
Int[j]=F ;

In this mechanism, an extra variable interested is used. This is a Boolean variable used to store the interest of the processes to get enter inside the critical section.

A process which wants to enter in the critical section first checks in the entry section whether the other process is interested to get inside. The process will wait for the time until the other process is interested.

In exit section, the process makes the value of its interest variable false so that the other process can get into the critical section.

The table shows the possible values of interest variable of both the processes and the process which get the chance in the scenario.

Interest [Pi]	Interest [Pj]	Process which get the chance
True	True	The process which first shows interest.
True	False	P_i
False	True	P_j
False	False	X

Let's analyze the mechanism on the basis of the requirements.

Mutual Exclusion
In interested variable mechanism, if one process is interested in getting into the CPU then the other process will wait until it becomes uninterested. Therefore, more than one process can never be present in the critical section at the same time hence the mechanism guarantees mutual exclusion.

Progress

In this mechanism, if a process is not interested in getting into the critical section then it will not stop the other process from getting into the critical section. Therefore the progress will definitely be provided by this method.

Bounded Waiting

To analyze bounded waiting, let us consider two processes Pi and Pj, are the cooperative processes wants to execute in the critical section. The instructions executed by the processes are shown below in relative manner.

Process Pi	Process Pj	Process Pi	Process Pj
1. Int [Pi] = True	1. Int [Pj] = True	1. Int [Pi] = False	1. While (Int [Pi] == True);
2. while (Int [Pj] == True);	2. while	2. Int [Pi] = True	//waiting for Pj
3. Critical Section	(Int[Pi]==True);	3. while (Int [Pj] == True);	
		//waiting for Pj	

Initially, the interest variable of both the processes is false. The process Pi shows the interest to get inside the critical section.

It sets its Interest Variable to true and check whether the Pj is also interested or not. Since the other process's interest variable is false hence Pi will get enter into the critical section.

Meanwhile, the process Pi is preempted and Pj is scheduled. Pj is a cooperative process and therefore, it also wants to enter in the critical section. It shows its interest by setting the interest variable to true.

It also checks whether the other process is also interested or not. We should notice that Pi is preempted but its interested variable is true that means it needs to further execute in the critical section. Therefore Pj will not get the chance and gets stuck in the while loop. Meanwhile, CPU changes Pi's state from blocked to running. Pi is yet to finish its critical section hence it finishes the critical section and makes an exit by setting the interest variable to False.

Now, a case can be possible when Pi again wants to enter in the critical section and set its interested variable to true and checks whether the interested variable of Pj is true. Here, Pj's interest variable is True hence Pi will get stuck in the while loop and waits for Pj become uninterested.

Since, Pj still stuck in the while loop waiting for the Pi' interested variable to become false. Therefore, both the processes are waiting for each other and none of them is getting into the critical section. This is a condition of deadlock and bounded waiting can never be provided in the case of deadlock.

Therefore, we can say that the interested variable mechanism doesn't guarantee deadlock.

Architectural Neutrality

The mechanism is a complete software mechanism executed in the user mode therefore it guarantees portability or architectural neutrality.

Mutual Exclusion	✓
Progress	✓
Bounded Waiting	✗
Portability	✓

Peterson's Solution

This is a software mechanism implemented at user mode. It is a busy waiting solution can be implemented for only two processes. It uses two variables that are turn variable and interested variable.

The Code of the solution is given below:
```
# define N 2
# define TRUE 1
# define FALSE 0
int interested[N] = FALSE;
int turn;
voidEntry_Section (int process)
```

```
{
    int other;
    other = 1-process;
    interested[process] = TRUE;
    turn = process;
    while (interested [other] =True && TURN=process);
}
voidExit_Section (int process)
{
    interested [process] = FALSE;
}
```

Till now, each of our solution is affected by one or the other problem. However, the Peterson solution provides you all the necessary requirements such as Mutual Exclusion, Progress, Bounded Waiting and Portability.

Analysis of Peterson Solution

```
voidEntry_Section (int process)
{
    int other;
    other = 1-process;
    interested[process] = TRUE;
    turn = process;
    while (interested [other] =True && TURN=process);
}
```

Critical Section

```
voidExit_Section (int process)
{
    interested [process] = FALSE;
}
```

This is a two process solution. Let us consider two cooperative processes P1 and P2. The entry section and exit section are shown below. Initially, the value of interested variables and turn variable is 0.

Initially process P1 arrives and wants to enter into the critical section. It sets its interested variable to True (instruction line 3) and also sets turn to 1 (line number 4). Since the condition given in line number 5 is completely satisfied by P1 therefore it will enter in the critical section.

P1 → 1 2 3 4 5 CS

Meanwhile, Process P1 got preempted and process P2 got scheduled. P2 also wants to enter in the critical section and executes instructions 1, 2, 3 and 4 of entry section. On instruction 5, it got stuck since it doesn't satisfy the condition (value of other interested variable is still true). Therefore it gets into the busy waiting.

P2 → 1 2 3 4 5

P1 again got scheduled and finish the critical section by executing the instruction no. 6 (setting interested variable to false). Now if P2 checks then it are going to satisfy the condition since other process's interested variable becomes false. P2 will also get enter the critical section.

P1 → 6
P2 → 5 CS

Any of the process may enter in the critical section for multiple numbers of times. Hence the procedure occurs in the cyclic order.

Mutual Exclusion
The method provides mutual exclusion for sure. In entry section, the while condition involves the criteria for two variables therefore a process cannot enter in the critical section until the other process is interested and the process is the last one to update turn variable.

Progress

An uninterested process will never stop the other interested process from entering in the critical section. If the other process is also interested then the process will wait.

Bounded waiting

The interested variable mechanism failed because it was not providing bounded waiting. However, in Peterson solution, A deadlock can never happen because the process which first sets the turn variable will enter in the critical section for sure. Therefore, if a process is preempted after executing line number 4 of the entry section then it will definitely get into the critical section in its next chance.

Portability

This is the complete software solution and therefore it is portable on every hardware.

Mutual Exclusion	✓
Progress	✓
Bounded Waiting	✓
Portability	✓

Synchronization Mechanism without busy waiting

All the solutions we have seen till now were intended to provide mutual exclusion with busy waiting. However, busy waiting is not the optimal allocation of resources because it keeps CPU busy all the time in checking the while loops condition continuously although the process is waiting for the critical section to become available.

All the synchronization mechanism with busy waiting are also suffering from the priority inversion problem that is there is always a possibility of spin lock whenever there is a process with the higher priority has to wait outside the critical section since the mechanism intends to execute the lower priority process in the critical section.

However these problems need a proper solution without busy waiting and priority inversion.

Sleep and Wake

(Producer Consumer problem)
Let's examine the basic model that is sleep and wake. Assume that we have two system calls as sleep and wake. The process which calls sleep will get blocked while the process which calls will get waked up.
There is a popular example called producer consumer problem which is the most popular problem simulating sleep and wake mechanism.

The concept of sleep and wake is very simple. If the critical section is not empty then the process will go and sleep. It will be waked up by the other process which is currently executing inside the critical section so that the process can get inside the critical section.

In producer consumer problem, let us say there are two processes, one process writes something while the other process reads that. The process which is writing something is called producer while the process which is reading is called consumer.

In order to read and write, both of them are using a buffer. The code that simulates the sleep and wake mechanism in terms of providing the solution to producer consumer problem is shown below.

```
#define N 100 //maximum slots in buffer
#define count=0 //items in the buffer
void producer (void)
{
    int item;
    while(True)
```

```
{
    item = produce_item(); //producer produces an item
    if(count == N) //if the buffer is full then the producer will sleep
        Sleep();
    insert_item (item); //the item is inserted into buffer
    countcount=count+1;
    if(count==1) //The producer will wake up the
    //consumer if there is at least 1 item in the buffer
    wake-up(consumer);
    }
}

void consumer (void)
{
    int item;
    while(True)
    {
        {
            if(count == 0) //The consumer will sleep if the buffer is empty.

            sleep();
            item = remove_item();
            countcount = count - 1;
            if(count == N-1)
//if there is at least one slot available in the buffer
        //then the consumer will wake up producer
            wake-up(producer);
            consume_item(item); //the item is read by consumer.
        }
    }
}
```

The producer produces the item and inserts it into the buffer. The value of the global variable count got increased at each insertion. If the buffer is filled completely and no slot is available then the producer will sleep, otherwise it keep inserting.

On the consumer's end, the value of count got decreased by 1 at each consumption. If the buffer is empty at any point of time then the consumer will sleep otherwise, it keeps consuming the items and decreasing the value of count by 1.

The consumer will be waked up by the producer if there is at least 1 item available in the buffer which is to be consumed. The producer will be waked up by the consumer if there is at least one slot available in the buffer so that the producer can write that.

Well, the problem arises in the case when the consumer got preempted just before it was about to sleep. Now the consumer is neither sleeping nor consuming. Since the producer is not aware of the fact that consumer is not actually sleeping therefore it keep waking the consumer while the consumer is not responding since it is not sleeping.
This leads to the wastage of system calls. When the consumer get scheduled again, it will sleep because it was about to sleep when it was preempted.

The producer keep writing in the buffer and it got filled after some time. The producer will also sleep at that time keeping in the mind that the consumer will wake him up when there is a slot available in the buffer.

The consumer is also sleeping and not aware with the fact that the producer will wake him up.

This is a kind of deadlock where neither producer nor consumer is active and waiting for each other to wake them up. This is a serious problem which needs to be addressed.

Using a flag bit to get rid of this problem
A flag bit can be used in order to get rid of this problem. The producer can set the bit when it calls wake-up on the first time. When the consumer got scheduled, it checks the bit.

The consumer will now get to know that the producer tried to wake him and therefore it will not sleep and get into the ready state to consume whatever produced by the producer.

This solution works for only one pair of producer and consumer, what if there are n producers and n consumers. In that case, there is a need to maintain an integer which can record how many wake-up calls have been made and how many consumers need not sleep. This integer variable is called semaphore. We will discuss more about semaphore later in detail.

Semaphore

To get rid of the problem of wasting the wake-up signals, Dijkstra proposed an approach which involves storing all the wake-up calls. Dijkstra states that, instead of giving the wake-up calls directly to the consumer, producer can store the wake-up call in a variable. Any of the consumers can read it whenever it needs to do so.

Semaphore is the variables which stores the entire wake up calls that are being transferred from producer to consumer. It is a variable on which read, modify and update happens automatically in kernel mode.

Semaphore cannot be implemented in the user mode because race condition may always arise when two or more processes try to access the variable simultaneously. It always needs support from the operating system to be implemented.

According to the demand of the situation, Semaphore can be divided into two categories.

1. Counting Semaphore
2. Binary Semaphore or Mutex

Counting Semaphore

There are the scenarios in which more than one processes need to execute in critical section simultaneously. However, counting semaphore can be used when we need to have more than one process in the critical section at the same time.

The programming code of semaphore implementation is shown below which includes the structure of semaphore and the logic using which the entry and the exit can be performed in the critical section.

```
struct Semaphore
{
    int value; // processes that can enter in the critical section simultan
eously.
    queue type L; // L contains set of processes which get blocked
}
Down (Semaphore S)
{
    SS.value = S.value -
1; //semaphore's value will get decreased when a new
    //process enter in the critical section
    if (S.value< 0)
    {
        put_process(PCB) in L; //if the value is negative then
        //the process will get into the blocked state.
        Sleep();
    }
    else
        return;
}
up (Semaphore s)
{
    SS.value = S.value+1; //semaphore value will get increased when
    //it makes an exit from the critical section.
    if(S.value<=0)
    {
        select a process from L; //if the value of semaphore is positive
        //then wake one of the processes in the blocked queue.
        wake-up();
    }
    }
}
```

In this mechanism, the entry and exit in the critical section are performed on the basis of the value of counting semaphore. The value of counting semaphore at any point of time indicates the maximum number of processes that can enter in the critical section at the same time.

A process which wants to enter in the critical section first decrease the semaphore value by 1 and then check whether it gets negative or not. If it gets negative then the process is pushed in the list of blocked processes (i.e. q) otherwise it gets enter in the critical section.

When a process exits from the critical section, it increases the counting semaphore by 1 and then checks whether it is negative or zero. If it is negative then that means that at least one process is waiting in the blocked state hence, to ensure bounded waiting, the first process among the list of blocked processes will wake up and gets enter in the critical section.

The processes in the blocked list will get waked in the order in which they slept. If the value of counting semaphore is negative then it states the number of processes in the blocked state while if it is positive then it states the number of slots available in the critical section.

Problem on Counting Semaphore

The questions are being asked on counting semaphore in GATE. Generally the questions are very simple that contains only subtraction and addition.

Wait → Decre → Down → P
Signal → Inc → Up → V

The following type questions can be asked in GATE.
A Counting Semaphore was initialized to 12, then 10P (wait) and 4V (Signal) operations were computed on this semaphore. What is the result?

$S = 12$ (initial)
10 p (wait) :
$SS = S - 10 = 12 - 10 = 2$
then 4 V :

SS = S + 4 = 2 + 4 = 6
Hence, the final value of counting semaphore is 6.

Binary Semaphore or Mutex

In counting semaphore, Mutual exclusion was not provided because we has the set of processes which required to execute in the critical section simultaneously.

However, Binary Semaphore strictly provides mutual exclusion. Here, instead of having more than 1 slots available in the critical section, we can only have at most 1 process in the critical section. The semaphore can have only two values, 0 or 1.
Let's see the programming implementation of Binary Semaphore.

StructBsemaphore
{
    enum Value(0,1); //value is enumerated data type which can only h
ave two values 0 or 1.
    Queue type L;
}
/* L contains all PCBs corresponding to process
Blocked while processing down operation unsuccessfully.
*/
Down (Bsemaphore S)
{
    if (s.value == 1) // if a slot is available in the
    //critical section then let the process enter in the queue.
    {
        S.value = 0; // initialize the value to 0 so that no other process ca
n read it as 1.
    }
    else
    {
        put the process (PCB) in S.L; //if no slot is available
        //then let the process wait in the blocked queue.
        sleep();
    }
}
Up (Bsemaphore S)

```
{
    if (S.L is empty) //an empty blocked processes list implies that no p
rocess
    //has ever tried to get enter in the critical section.
    {
        S.Value =1;
    }
    else
    {
        Select a process from S.L;
        Wakeup(); // if it is not empty then wake the first process of the
blocked queue.
    }
}
```

Chapter 5 - Deadlock

Every process needs some resources to complete its execution. However, the resource is granted in a sequential order.

1. The process requests for some resource.

2. OS grant the resource if it is available otherwise let the process waits.

3. The process uses it and release on the completion.

A Deadlock is a situation where each of the computer process waits for a resource which is being assigned to some another process. In this situation, none of the process gets executed since the resource it needs, is held by some other process which is also waiting for some other resource to be released.

Let us assume that there are three processes P1, P2 and P3. There are three different resources R1, R2 and R3. R1 is assigned to P1, R2 is assigned to P2 and R3 is assigned to P3.

After some time, P1 demands for R1 which is being used by P2. P1 halts its execution since it can't complete without R2. P2 also demands for R3 which is being used by P3. P2 also stops its execution because it can't continue without R3. P3 also demands for R1 which is being used by P1 therefore P3 also stops its execution.

In this scenario, a cycle is being formed among the three processes. None of the process is progressing and they are all waiting. The computer becomes unresponsive since all the processes got blocked.

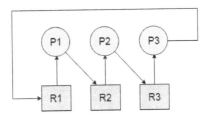

Difference between Starvation and Deadlock

Deadlock	Starvation
Deadlock is a situation where no process got blocked and no process proceeds	Starvation is a situation where the low priority process got blocked and the high priority processes proceed.
Deadlock is an infinite waiting.	Starvation is a long waiting but not infinite.
Every Deadlock is always a starvation.	Every starvation need not be deadlock.
The requested resource is blocked by the other process.	The requested resource is continuously be used by the higher priority processes.
Deadlock happens when Mutual exclusion, hold and wait, No preemption and circular wait occurs simultaneously.	It occurs due to the uncontrolled priority and resource management.

Conditions for Deadlock

Mutual Exclusion
A resource can only be shared in mutually exclusive manner. It implies, two process cannot use the same resource at the same time.

Hold and Wait

A process waits for some resources while holding another resource at the same time.

No preemption
The process which once scheduled will be executed till the completion. No other process can be scheduled by the scheduler meanwhile.

Circular Wait
All the processes must be waiting for the resources in a cyclic manner so that the last process is waiting for the resource which is being held by the first process.

Strategies for handling Deadlock

1. Deadlock Ignorance
Deadlock Ignorance is the most widely used approach among all the mechanism. This is being used by many operating systems mainly for end user uses. In this approach, the Operating system assumes that deadlock never occurs. It simply ignores deadlock. This approach is best suitable for a single end user system where User uses the system only for browsing and all other normal stuff.

There is always a tradeoff between Correctness and performance. The operating systems like Windows and Linux mainly focus upon performance. However, the performance of the system decreases if it uses deadlock handling mechanism all the time if deadlock happens 1 out of 100 times then it is completely unnecessary to use the deadlock handling mechanism all the time.

In these types of systems, the user has to simply restart the computer in the case of deadlock. Windows and Linux are mainly using this approach.

2. Deadlock prevention
Deadlock happens only when Mutual Exclusion, hold and wait, No preemption and circular wait holds simultaneously. If it is possible to violate one of the four conditions at any time then the deadlock can never occur in the system.

The idea behind the approach is very simple that we have to fail one of the four conditions but there can be a big argument on its physical implementation in the system.

3. Deadlock avoidance

In deadlock avoidance, the operating system checks whether the system is in safe state or in unsafe state at every step which the operating system performs. The process continues until the system is in safe state. Once the system moves to unsafe state, the OS has to backtrack one step.

In simple words, The OS reviews each allocation so that the allocation doesn't cause the deadlock in the system.

4. Deadlock detection and recovery

This approach let the processes fall in deadlock and then periodically check whether deadlock occur in the system or not. If it occurs then it applies some of the recovery methods to the system to get rid of deadlock.

Deadlock Prevention

If we simulate deadlock with a table which is standing on its four legs then we can also simulate four legs with the four conditions which when occurs simultaneously, cause the deadlock.

However, if we break one of the legs of the table then the table will fall definitely. The same happens with deadlock, if we can be able to violate one of the four necessary conditions and don't let them occur together then we can prevent the deadlock.

Let's see how we can prevent each of the conditions.

1. Mutual Exclusion

Mutual section from the resource point of view is the fact that a resource can never be used by more than one process simultaneously which is fair enough but that is the main reason behind the deadlock. If a resource could have been used by more than one process at the same time then the process would have never been waiting for any resource.

However, if we can be able to violate resources behaving in the mutually exclusive manner then the deadlock can be prevented.

Spooling

For a device like printer, spooling can work. There is a memory associated with the printer which stores jobs from each of the process into it. Later, Printer collects all the jobs and print each one of them according to FCFS. By using this mechanism, the process doesn't have to wait for the printer and it can continue whatever it was doing. Later, it collects the output when it is produced.

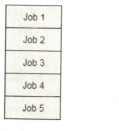

Spool

Although, Spooling can be an effective approach to violate mutual exclusion but it suffers from two kinds of problems.

1. This cannot be applied to every resource.

2. After some point of time, there may arise a race condition between the processes to get space in that spool.

We cannot force a resource to be used by more than one process at the same time since it will not be fair enough and some serious problems may arise in the performance. Therefore, we cannot violate mutual exclusion for a process practically.

2. Hold and Wait

Hold and wait condition lies when a process holds a resource and waiting for some other resource to complete its task. Deadlock occurs because there can be more than one process which are holding one resource and waiting for other in the cyclic order.

However, we have to find out some mechanism by which a process either doesn't hold any resource or doesn't wait. That means, a process must be assigned all the necessary resources before the execution starts. A process must not wait for any resource once the execution has been started.

!(Hold and wait) = !hold or !wait
(negation of hold and wait is, either you don't hold or you don't wait)

This can be implemented practically if a process declares all the resources initially. However, this sounds very practical but can't be done in the computer system because a process can't determine necessary resources initially.

Process is the set of instructions which are executed by the CPU. Each of the instruction may demand multiple resources at the multiple times. The need cannot be fixed by the OS.
The problem with the approach is:
1. Practically not possible.
2. Possibility of getting starved will be increases due to the fact that some process may hold a resource for a very long time.

3. No Preemption
Deadlock arises due to the fact that a process can't be stopped once it starts. However, if we take the resource away from the process which is causing deadlock then we can prevent deadlock.

This is not a good approach at all since if we take a resource away which is being used by the process then all the work which it has done till now can become inconsistent.

Consider a printer is being used by any process. If we take the printer away from that process and assign it to some other process then all the data which has been printed can become inconsistent and ineffective and also the fact that the process can't start printing again from where it has left which causes performance inefficiency.

4. Circular Wait
To violate circular wait, we can assign a priority number to each of the resource. A process can't request for a lesser priority resource.

This ensures that not a single process can request a resource which is being utilized by some other process and no cycle will be formed.

Condition	Approach	Is Practically Possible?
Mutual Exclusion	Spooling	✗
Hold and Wait	Request for all the resources initially	✗
No Preemption	Snatch all the resources	✗
Circular Wait	Assign priority to each resources and order resources numerically	✓

Among all the methods, violating Circular wait is the only approach that can be implemented practically.

Deadlock Avoidance

In deadlock avoidance, the request for any resource will be granted if the resulting state of the system doesn't cause deadlock in the system. The state of the system will continuously be checked for safe and unsafe states.

In order to avoid deadlocks, the process must tell OS, the maximum number of resources a process can request to complete its execution.

The simplest and most useful approach states that the process should declare the maximum number of resources of each type it may ever need. The Deadlock avoidance algorithm examines the resource allocations so that there can never be a circular wait condition.

Safe and Unsafe States

The resource allocation state of a system can be defined by the instances of available and allocated resources, and the maximum instance of the resources demanded by the processes.

A state of a system recorded at some random time is shown below.

Resources Assigned

Process	Type 1	Type 2	Type 3	Type 4
A	3	0	2	2
B	0	0	1	1
C	1	1	1	0
D	2	1	4	0

Resources still needed

Process	Type 1	Type 2	Type 3	Type 4
A	1	1	0	0
B	0	1	1	2
C	1	2	1	0
D	2	1	1	2

$E = (7\ 6\ 8\ 4)$
$P = (6\ 2\ 8\ 3)$
$A = (1\ 4\ 0\ 1)$

Above tables and vector E, P and A describes the resource allocation state of a system. There are 4 processes and 4 types of the resources in a system. Table 1 shows the instances of each resource assigned to each process.

Table 2 shows the instances of the resources, each process still needs. Vector E is the representation of total instances of each resource in the system.

Vector P represents the instances of resources that have been assigned to processes. Vector A represents the number of resources that are not in use.

A state of the system is called safe if the system can allocate all the resources requested by all the processes without entering into deadlock.

If the system cannot fulfill the request of all processes then the state of the system is called unsafe.

The key of Deadlock avoidance approach is when the request is made for resources then the request must only be approved in the case if the resulting state is also a safe state.

Resource Allocation Graph

The resource allocation graph is the pictorial representation of the state of a system. As its name suggests, the resource allocation graph is the complete information about all the processes which are holding some resources or waiting for some resources.

It also contains the information about all the instances of all the resources whether they are available or being used by the processes.

In Resource allocation graph, the process is represented by a Circle while the Resource is represented by a rectangle. Let's see the types of vertices and edges in detail.

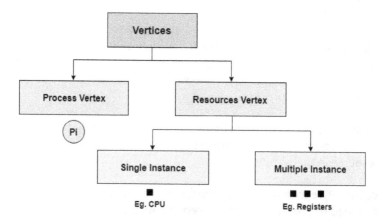

Vertices are mainly of two types, Resource and process. Each of them will be represented by a different shape. Circle represents process while rectangle represents resource.

A resource can have more than one instance. Each instance will be represented by a dot inside the rectangle.

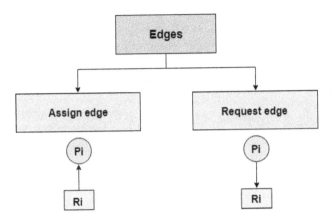

Edges in RAG are also of two types, one represents assignment and other represents the wait of a process for a resource. The above image shows each of them.

A resource is shown as assigned to a process if the tail of the arrow is attached to an instance to the resource and the head is attached to a process.

A process is shown as waiting for a resource if the tail of an arrow is attached to the process while the head is pointing towards the resource.

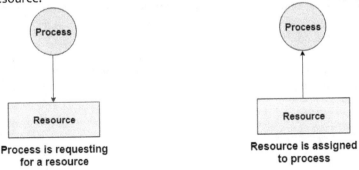

Process is requesting   Resource is assigned
for a resource   to process

Example

Let's consider 3 processes P1, P2 and P3, and two types of resources R1 and R2. The resources are having 1 instance each.

According to the graph, R1 is being used by P1, P2 is holding R2 and waiting for R1, P3 is waiting for R1 as well as R2.

The graph is deadlock free since no cycle is being formed in the graph.

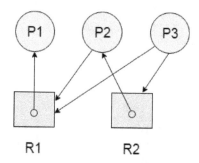

Deadlock Detection using RAG

If a cycle is being formed in a Resource allocation graph where all the resources have the single instance then the system is deadlocked.

In Case of Resource allocation graph with multi-instanced resource types, Cycle is a necessary condition of deadlock but not the sufficient condition.

The following example contains three processes P1, P2, P3 and three resources R2, R2, R3. All the resources are having single instances each.

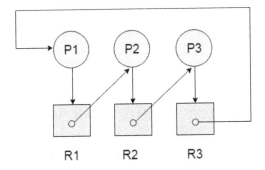

If we analyze the graph then we can find out that there is a cycle formed in the graph since the system is satisfying all the four conditions of deadlock.

Allocation Matrix

Allocation matrix can be formed by using the Resource allocation graph of a system. In Allocation matrix, an entry will be made for each of the resource assigned. For Example, in the following matrix, an entry is being made in front of P1 and below R3 since R3 is assigned to P1.

Process	R1	R2	R3
P1	0	0	1
P2	1	0	0
P3	0	1	0

Request Matrix

In request matrix, an entry will be made for each of the resource requested. As in the following example, P1 needs R1 therefore an entry is being made in front of P1 and below R1.

Process	R1	R2	R3
P1	1	0	0
P2	0	1	0
P3	0	0	1

Avial = (0,0,0)

We are neither having any resource available in the system nor a process going to release. Each of the process needs at least single resource to complete therefore they will continuously be holding each one of them.

We cannot fulfill the demand of at least one process using the available resources therefore the system is deadlocked as determined earlier when we detected a cycle in the graph.

Deadlock Detection and Recovery

In this approach, The OS doesn't apply any mechanism to avoid or prevent the deadlocks. Therefore the system considers that the deadlock will definitely occur. In order to get rid of deadlocks, The OS periodically checks the system for any deadlock. In case, it finds any of the deadlock then the OS will recover the system using some recovery techniques.

The main task of the OS is detecting the deadlocks. The OS can detect the deadlocks with the help of Resource allocation graph.

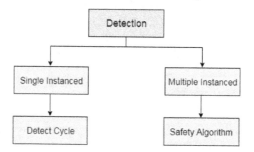

In single instanced resource types, if a cycle is being formed in the system then there will definitely be a deadlock. On the other hand, in multiple instanced resource type graph, detecting a cycle is not just enough. We have to apply the safety algorithm on the system by converting the resource allocation graph into the allocation matrix and request matrix.

In order to recover the system from deadlocks, either OS considers resources or processes.

1. Considering a Resource

Preempt the resource
We can snatch one of the resources from the owner of the resource (process) and give it to the other process with the expectation that it will complete the execution and will release this resource sooner. Well, choosing a resource which will be snatched is going to be a bit difficult.

Rollback to a safe state
System passes through various states to get into the deadlock state. The operating system can rollback the system to the previous safe state. For this purpose, OS needs to implement check pointing at every state.

The moment, we get into deadlock, we will rollback all the allocations to get into the previous safe state.

2. Considering a Process

Kill a process
Killing a process can solve our problem but the bigger concern is to decide which process to kill. Generally, Operating system kills a process which has done least amount of work until now.

Kill all process
This is not a suggestible approach but can be implemented if the problem becomes very serious. Killing all process will lead to inefficiency in the system because all the processes will execute again from starting.

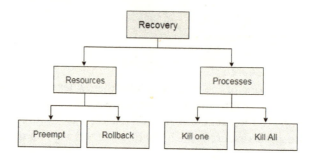

Chapter 6 - Memory

Management

What is Memory?

Computer memory can be defined as a collection of some data represented in the binary format. On the basis of various functions, memory can be classified into various categories. We will discuss each one of them later in detail.

A computer device that is capable to store any information or data temporally or permanently, is called storage device.

How Data is being stored in a computer system?

In order to understand memory management, we have to make everything clear about how data is being stored in a computer system. The machine understands only binary language that is 0 or 1. Computer converts every data into binary language first and then stores it into the memory.

That means if we have a program line written as int α = 10 then the computer converts it into the binary language and then store it into the memory blocks.

The representation of int i = 10 is shown below.

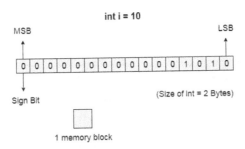

The binary representation of 10 is 1010. Here, we are considering 32 bit system therefore, the size of int is 2 bytes i.e. 16 bit. 1 memory block stores 1 bit. If we are using signed integer then the most significant bit in the memory array is always a signed bit.

Signed bit value 0 represents positive integer while 1 represents negative integer. Here, the range of values that can be stored using the memory array is -32768 to +32767.

well, we can enlarge this range by using unsigned int. in that case, the bit which is now storing the sign will also store the bit value and therefore the range will be 0 to 65,535.

Need for Multi programming

However, The CPU can directly access the main memory, Registers and cache of the system. The program always executes in main memory. The size of main memory affects degree of Multi programming to most of the extant. If the size of the main memory is larger than CPU can load more processes in the main memory at the same time and therefore will increase degree of Multi programming as well as CPU utilization.

Let's consider,
Process Size = 4 MB
Main memory size = 4 MB
The process can only reside in the main memory at any time.
If the time for which the process does IO is P,

Then,
 CPU utilization = (1-P)
let's say,
P = 70%
CPU utilization = 30 %
Now, increase the memory size, Let's say it is 8 MB.
Process Size = 4 MB
Two processes can reside in the main memory at the same time.
Let's say the time for which, one process does its IO is P,

Then,
CPU utilization = $(1-P^2)$
let's say P = 70 %
CPU utilization = (1-0.49) =0.51 = 51 %

Therefore, we can state that the CPU utilization will be increased if the memory size gets increased.

Fixed Partitioning

The earliest and one of the simplest technique which can be used to load more than one processes into the main memory is Fixed partitioning or Contiguous memory allocation.

In this technique, the main memory is divided into partitions of equal or different sizes. The operating system always resides in the first partition while the other partitions can be used to store user processes. The memory is assigned to the processes in contiguous way.

In fixed partitioning,

1. The partitions cannot overlap.
2. A process must be contiguously present in a partition for the execution.

There are various cons of using this technique.

1. Internal Fragmentation
If the size of the process is lesser then the total size of the partition then some size of the partition get wasted and remain unused. This is wastage of the memory and called internal fragmentation.

As shown in the image below, the 4 MB partition is used to load only 3 MB process and the remaining 1 MB got wasted.

2. External Fragmentation
The total unused space of various partitions cannot be used to load the processes even though there is space available but not in the contiguous form.
As shown in the image below, the remaining 1 MB space of each partition cannot be used as a unit to store a 4 MB process. Despite of the fact that the sufficient space is available to load the process, process will not be loaded.

3. Limitation on the size of the process
If the process size is larger than the size of maximum sized partition then that process cannot be loaded into the memory. Therefore, a limitation can be imposed on the process size that is it cannot be larger than the size of the largest partition.

4. Degree of multiprogramming is less
By Degree of multi programming, we simply mean the maximum number of processes that can be loaded into the memory at the same time. In fixed partitioning, the degree of multiprogramming is fixed and very less due to the fact that the size of the partition cannot be varied according to the size of processes.

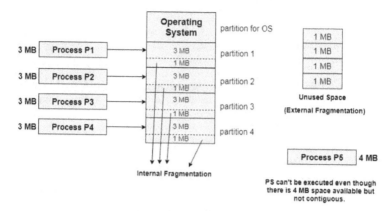

Fixed Partitioning

(Contiguous memory allocation)

Dynamic Partitioning

Dynamic partitioning tries to overcome the problems caused by fixed partitioning. In this technique, the partition size is not declared initially. It is declared at the time of process loading.

The first partition is reserved for the operating system. The remaining space is divided into parts. The size of each partition will be equal to the size of the process. The partition size varies according to the need of the process so that the internal fragmentation can be avoided.

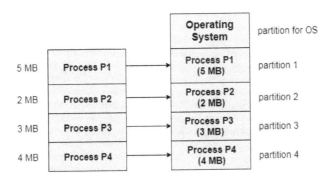

Dynamic Partitioning

(Process Size = Partition Size)

Advantages of Dynamic Partitioning over fixed partitioning

1. No Internal Fragmentation

Given the fact that the partitions in dynamic partitioning are created according to the need of the process, It is clear that there will not be any internal fragmentation because there will not be any unused remaining space in the partition.

2. No Limitation on the size of the process

In Fixed partitioning, the process with the size greater than the size of the largest partition could not be executed due to the lack of sufficient contiguous memory. Here, In Dynamic partitioning, the process size can't be restricted since the partition size is decided according to the process size.

3. Degree of multiprogramming is dynamic

Due to the absence of internal fragmentation, there will not be any unused space in the partition hence more processes can be loaded in the memory at the same time.

Disadvantages of dynamic partitioning

External Fragmentation

Absence of internal fragmentation doesn't mean that there will not be external fragmentation.

Let's consider three processes P1 (1 MB) and P2 (3 MB) and P3 (1 MB) are being loaded in the respective partitions of the main memory.

After some time P1 and P3 got completed and their assigned space is freed. Now there are two unused partitions (1 MB and 1 MB) available in the main memory but they cannot be used to load a 2 MB process in the memory since they are not contiguously located.

The rule says that the process must be contiguously present in the main memory to get executed. We need to change this rule to avoid external fragmentation.

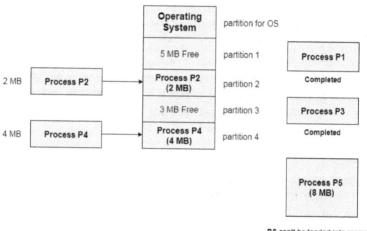

External Fragmentation in
Dynamic Partitioning

Complex Memory Allocation

In Fixed partitioning, the list of partitions is made once and will never change but in dynamic partitioning, the allocation and deallocation is very complex since the partition size will be varied every time when it is assigned to a new process. OS has to keep track of all the partitions.

Due to the fact that the allocation and deallocation are done very frequently in dynamic memory allocation and the partition size will be changed at each time, it is going to be very difficult for OS to manage everything.

Compaction

We got to know that the dynamic partitioning suffers from external fragmentation. However, this can cause some serious problems.
To avoid compaction, we need to change the rule which says that the process can't be stored in the different places in the memory.
We can also use compaction to minimize the probability of external fragmentation. In compaction, all the free partitions are made contiguous and all the loaded partitions are brought together.
By applying this technique, we can store the bigger processes in the memory. The free partitions are merged which can now be allocated according to the needs of new processes. This technique is also called defragmentation.

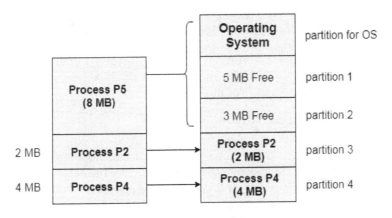

Now P5 can be loaded into memory
because the free space is now made
contiguous by compaction

Compaction

As shown in the image above, the process P5, which could not be loaded into the memory due to the lack of contiguous space, can be loaded now in the memory since the free partitions are made contiguous.

Problem with Compaction

The efficiency of the system is decreased in the case of compaction due to the fact that all the free spaces will be transferred from several places to a single place.

Huge amount of time is invested for this procedure and the CPU will remain idle for all this time. Despite of the fact that the compaction avoids external fragmentation, it makes system inefficient.

Let us consider that OS needs 6 NS to copy 1 byte from one place to another.

1. 1 B transfer needs 6 NS

2. 256 MB transfer needs 256 X 2^20 X 6 X 10 ^ -9 secs

Hence, it is proved to some extent that the larger size memory transfer needs some huge amount of time that is in seconds.

Bit Map for Dynamic Partitioning

The Main concern for dynamic partitioning is keeping track of all the free and allocated partitions. However, the Operating system uses following data structures for this task.

1. Bit Map

2. Linked List

Bit Map is the least famous data structure to store the details. In this scheme, the main memory is divided into the collection of allocation units. One or more allocation units may be allocated to a process according to the need of that process. However, the size of the allocation unit is fixed that is defined by the Operating System and never changed. Although the partition size may vary but the allocation size is fixed.

The main task of the operating system is to keep track of whether the partition is free or filled. For this purpose, the operating system also manages another data structure that is called bitmap.

The process or the hole in Allocation units is represented by a flag bit of bitmap. In the image shown below, a flag bit is defined for every bit of allocation units. However, it is not the general case, it depends on the OS that, for how many bits of the allocation units, it wants to store the flag bit.

The flag bit is set to 1 if there is a contiguously present process at the adjacent bit in allocation unit otherwise it is set to 0.
A string of 0s in the bitmap shows that there is a hole in the relative Allocation unit while the string of 1s represents the process in the relative allocation unit.

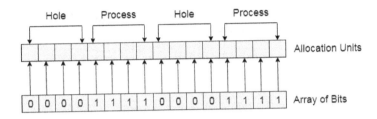

1 Allocation Unit = 1/2 byte

1 Bit of Bit Map ⟶ 1 Bit of Allocation Unit

1/5 of the total memory is taken by Bit Map

0 ⟶ Hole

0 ⟶ Process

Bit Map for Dynamic Partitioning

Disadvantages of using Bitmap
1. The OS has to assign some memory for bitmap as well since it stores the details about allocation units. That much amount of memory cannot be used to load any process therefore that decreases the degree of multiprogramming as well as throughput.

In the above image,
The allocation unit is of 4 bits that is 0.5 bits. Here, 1 bit of the bitmap is representing 1 bit of allocation unit.
a)   Size of 1 allocation unit = 4 bits

b) Size of bitmap = 1/(4+1) = 1/5 of total main memory.
Therefore, in this bitmap configuration, 1/5 of total main memory is wasted.

2. To identify any hole in the memory, the OS need to search the string of os in the bitmap. This searching takes a huge amount of time which makes the system inefficient to some extent.

Linked List for Dynamic Partitioning

The better and the most popular approach to keep track the free or filled partitions is using Linked List.

In this approach, the Operating system maintains a linked list where each node represents each partition. Every node has three fields.

1. First field of the node stores a flag bit which shows whether the partition is a hole or some process is inside.
2. Second field stores the starting index of the partition.
3. Third filed stores the end index of the partition.

If a partition is freed at some point of time then that partition will be merged with its adjacent free partition without doing any extra effort.

There are some points which need to be focused while using this approach.

1. The OS must be very clear about the location of the new node which is to be added in the linked list. However, adding the node according to the increasing order of starting index is suggestible.
2. Using a doubly linked list will make some positive effects on the performance due to the fact that a node in the doubly link list can also keep track of its previous node.

Linked List for Dynamic Partitioning

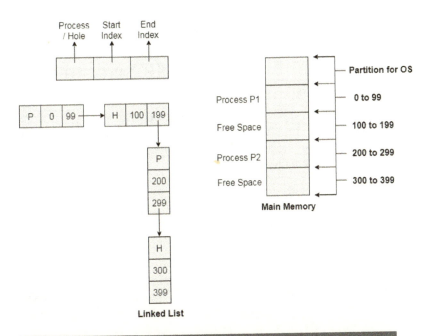

Linked List

Main Memory

Partitioning Algorithms

There are various algorithms which are implemented by the Operating System in order to find out the holes in the linked list and allocate them to the processes.

The explanation about each of the algorithm is given below.

1. First Fit Algorithm

First Fit algorithm scans the linked list and whenever it finds the first big enough hole to store a process, it stops scanning and load the process into that hole. This procedure produces two partitions. Out of them, one partition will be a hole while the other partition will store the process.

First Fit algorithm maintains the linked list according to the increasing order of starting index. This is the simplest to implement among all the algorithms and produces bigger holes as compare to the other algorithms.

2. Next Fit Algorithm

Next Fit algorithm is similar to First Fit algorithm except the fact that, Next fit scans the linked list from the node where it previously allocated a hole.

Next fit doesn't scan the whole list, it starts scanning the list from the next node. The idea behind the next fit is the fact that the list has been scanned once therefore the probability of finding the hole is larger in the remaining part of the list.

Experiments over the algorithm have shown that the next fit is not better than the first fit, so it is not being used these days in most of the cases.

3. Best Fit Algorithm

The Best Fit algorithm tries to find out the smallest hole possible in the list that can accommodate the size requirement of the process. Using Best Fit has some disadvantages.

1. 1. It is slower because it scans the entire list every time and tries to find out the smallest hole which can satisfy the requirement the process.

2. Due to the fact that the difference between the whole size and the process size is very small, the holes produced will be as small as it cannot be used to load any process and therefore it remains useless.

   Despite of the fact that the name of the algorithm is best fit, it is not the best algorithm among all.

4. Worst Fit Algorithm

The worst fit algorithm scans the entire list every time and tries to find out the biggest hole in the list which can fulfill the requirement of the process.

Despite of the fact that this algorithm produces the larger holes to load the other processes, this is not the better approach due to the fact that it is slower because it searches the entire list every time again and again.

5. Quick Fit Algorithm
The quick fit algorithm suggests maintaining the different lists of frequently used sizes. Although, it is not practically suggestible because the procedure takes so much time to create the different lists and then expending the holes to load a process.

The first fit algorithm is the best algorithm among all because:

1. It takes lesser time compare to the other algorithms.
2. It produces bigger holes that can be used to load other processes later on.
3. It is easiest to implement.

GATE question on best fit and first fit
From the GATE point of view, Numerical on best fit and first fit are being asked frequently in 1 mark. Let's have a look on the one given as below.

Process requests are given as:
25 K, 50 K, 100 K, 75 K

| 50 K | 75 K | 150 K | 175 K | 300 K |

Determine the algorithm which can optimally satisfy this requirement.

1. First Fit algorithm
2. Best Fit Algorithm
3. Neither of the two
4. Both of them

In the question, there are five partitions in the memory. 3 partitions are having processes inside them and two partitions are holes.
Our task is to check the algorithm which can satisfy the request optimally.

First Fit Algorithm

Let's see, how first fit algorithm works on this problem.

1. 25 K requirement

The algorithm scans the list until it gets first hole which should be big enough to satisfy the request of 25 K. it gets the space in the second partition which is free hence it allocates 25 K out of 75 K to the process and the remaining 50 K is produced as hole.

50 K	50K	150 K	175 K	300 K
◯	○	◯		◯

25K

2. 50 K requirement

The 50 K requirement can be fulfilled by allocating the third partition which is 50 K in size to the process. No free space is produced as free space.

50 K		150 K	175 K	300 K
◯	○	◯		◯

25K 50K

3. 100 K requirement

100 K requirement can be fulfilled by using the fifth partition of 175 K size. Out of 175 K, 100 K will be allocated and remaining 75 K will be there as a hole.

50 K		150 K	75 K	300 K
◯	○	◯	◯	◯

25K 50K   100K

4. 75 K requirement

Since we are having a 75 K free partition hence we can allocate that much space to the process which is demanding just 75 K space.

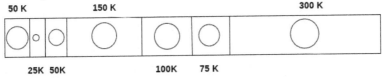

Using first fit algorithm, we have fulfilled the entire request optimally and no useless space is remaining.

Let's see, How Best Fit algorithm performs for the problem.

Best Fit Algorithm

1. 25 K requirement

To allocate 25 K space using best fit approach, need to scan the whole list and then we find that a 75 K partition is free and the smallest among all, which can accommodate the need of the process.

Therefore 25 K out of those 75 K free partition is allocated to the process and the remaining 50 K is produced as a hole.

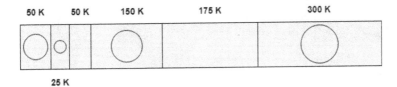

2. 50 K requirement

To satisfy this need, we will again scan the whole list and then find the 50 K space is free which the exact match of the need is. Therefore, it will be allocated for the process.

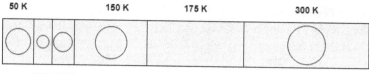

3. 100 K requirement

100 K need is close enough to the 175 K space. The algorithm scans the whole list and then allocates 100 K out of 175 K from the 5th free partition.

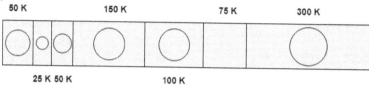

4. 75 K requirement

75 K requirement will get the space of 75 K from the 6th free partition but the algorithm will scan the whole list in the process of taking this decision.

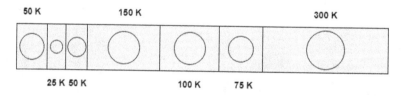

By following both of the algorithms, we have noticed that both the algorithms perform similar to most of the extant in this case.

Both can satisfy the need of the processes but however, the best fit algorithm scans the list again and again which takes lot of time.

Therefore, if you ask me that which algorithm performs in more optimal way then it will be **First Fit algorithm** for sure.

Therefore, the answer in this case is A.

Paging

The main disadvantage of Dynamic Partitioning is External fragmentation. Although, this can be removed by Compaction but as we have discussed earlier, the compaction makes the system inefficient.

We need to find out a mechanism which can load the processes in the partitions in a more optimal way. Let us discuss a dynamic and flexible mechanism called paging.

Need for Paging

Consider a process P1 of size 2 MB and the main memory which is divided into three partitions. Out of the three partitions, two partitions are holes of size 1 MB each.

P1 needs 2 MB space in the main memory to be loaded. We have two holes of 1 MB each but they are not contiguous.

Although, there is 2 MB space available in the main memory in the form of those holes but that remains useless until it become contiguous. This is a serious problem to address.

We need to have some kind of mechanism which can store one process at different locations of the memory. The Idea behind paging is to divide the process in pages so that, we can store them in the memory at different holes. We will discuss paging with the examples in the next sections.

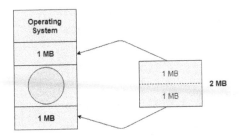

The process needs to be divided into two
parts to get stored at two different places.

Paging with Example

In Operating Systems, Paging is a storage mechanism used to retrieve processes from the secondary storage into the main memory in the form of pages.

The main idea behind the paging is to divide each process in the form of pages. The main memory will also be divided in the form of frames.

One page of the process is to be stored in one of the frames of the memory. The pages can be stored at the different locations of the memory but the priority is always to find the contiguous frames or holes.

Pages of the process are brought into the main memory only when they are required otherwise they reside in the secondary storage. Different operating system defines different frame sizes. The sizes of each frame must be equal. Considering the fact that the pages are mapped to the frames in Paging, page size needs to be as same as frame size.

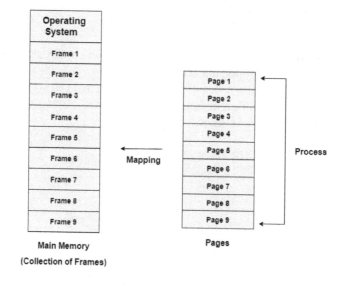

Example

Let us consider the main memory size 16 Kb and Frame size is 1 KB therefore the main memory will be divided into the collection of 16 frames of 1 KB each.

There are 4 processes in the system that is P1, P2, P3 and P4 of 4 KB each. Each process is divided into pages of 1 KB each so that one page can be stored in one frame.

Initially, all the frames are empty therefore pages of the processes will get stored in the contiguous way.

Frames, pages and the mapping between the two is shown in the image below.

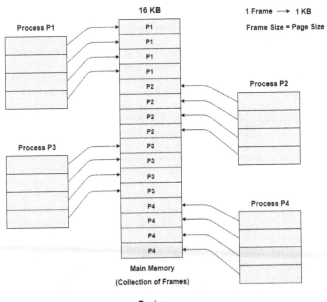

Paging

Let us consider that, P2 and P4 are moved to waiting state after some time. Now, 8 frames become empty and therefore other pages can be loaded in that empty place. The process P5 of size 8 KB (8 pages) is waiting inside the ready queue.

Given the fact that, we have 8 non-contiguous frames available in the memory and paging provides the flexibility of storing the process at the different places. Therefore, we can load the pages of process P5 in the place of P2 and P4.

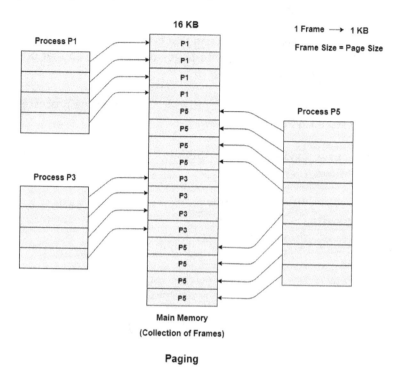

Paging

Memory Management Unit

The purpose of **Memory Management Unit (MMU)** is to convert the logical address into the physical address. The logical address is the address generated by the CPU for every page while the physical address is the actual address of the frame where each page will be stored.

When a page is to be accessed by the CPU by using the logical address, the operating system needs to obtain the physical address to access that page physically.

The logical address has two parts.

1.   Page Number

2. Offset

Memory management unit of OS needs to convert the page number to the frame number.

Example
Considering the above image, let's say that the CPU demands 10th word of 4th page of process P3. Since the page number 4 of process P1 gets stored at frame number 9 therefore the 10th word of 9th frame will be returned as the physical address.

Basics of Binary Addresses

Computer system assigns the binary addresses to the memory locations. However, the system uses amount of bits to address a memory location.

Using 1 bit, we can address two memory locations. Using 2 bits we can address 4 and using 3 bits we can address 8 memory locations.

A pattern can be identified in the mapping between the number of bits in the address and the range of the memory locations.

We know,
Using 1 Bit we can represent 2^1 i.e. 2 memory locations.
Using 2 bits, we can represent 2^2 i.e. 4 memory locations.
Using 3 bits, we can represent 2^3 i.e. 8 memory locations.

Therefore, if we generalize this,
Using n bits, we can assign 2^n memory locations.
n bits of address $\rightarrow$ 2^n memory locations

1 Bit	2 Bits	3 Bits
0	0 0	0 0 0
1	0 1	0 0 1
	1 0	0 1 0
	1 1	0 1 1
		1 0 0
		1 0 1
		1 1 0
		1 1 1

these n bits can be divided into two parts that are, K bits and (n-k) bits.

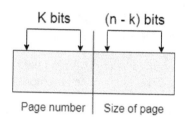

$$2^n = 2^n \times 2^{n-k}$$

Physical Address Space

Physical address space in a system can be defined as the size of the main memory. It is really important to compare the process size with the physical address space. The process size must be less than the physical address space.

Physical Address Space = Size of the Main Memory

If, physical address space = 64 KB = 2^6 KB = $2^6 \times 2^{10}$ bytes = 2^{16} bytes

Let us consider,
word size = 8 Bytes = 2^3 Bytes

Hence,
Physical address space (in words) = $(2^{16}) / (2^3) = 2^{13}$ Words

Therefore,
Physical Address = 13 bits

In General,
If, Physical Address Space = N Words

then, Physical Address = $\log_2 N$

Logical Address Space

Logical address space can be defined as the size of the process. The size of the process should be less enough so that it can reside in the main memory.

Let's say,
Logical Address Space = 128 MB = $(2^7 \times 2^{20})$ Bytes = 2^{27} Bytes
Word size = 4 Bytes = 2^2 Bytes

Logical Address Space (in words) = $(2^{27}) / (2^2) = 2^{25}$ Words
Logical Address = 25 Bits

In general,
If, logical address space = L words
Then, Logical Address = $\log_2 L$ bits

Word
The Word is the smallest unit of the memory. It is the collection of bytes. Every operating system defines different word sizes after analyzing the n-bit address that is inputted to the decoder and the 2^n memory locations that are produced from the decoder.

Page Table

Page Table is a data structure used by the virtual memory system to store the mapping between logical addresses and physical addresses.

Logical addresses are generated by the CPU for the pages of the processes therefore they are generally used by the processes.

Physical addresses are the actual frame address of the memory. They are generally used by the hardware or more specifically by RAM subsystems.

The image given below considers,

Physical Address Space = M words
Logical Address Space = L words
Page Size = P words

Physical Address = $\log_2 M$ = m bits
Logical Address = $\log_2 L$ = l bits
page offset = $\log_2 P$ = p bits

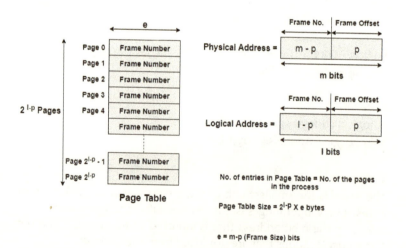

Page Table

Physical Address =

Logical Address =

No. of entries in Page Table = No. of the pages in the process

Page Table Size = 2^{l-p} X e bytes

e = m-p (Frame Size) bits

The CPU always accesses the processes through their logical addresses. However, the main memory recognizes physical address only.

In this situation, a unit named as Memory Management Unit comes into the picture. It converts the page number of the logical address to the frame number of the physical address. The offset remains same in both the addresses.

To perform this task, Memory Management unit needs a special kind of mapping which is done by page table. The page table stores all the Frame numbers corresponding to the page numbers of the page table.

In other words, the page table maps the page number to its actual location (frame number) in the memory.

In the image given below shows, how the required word of the frame is accessed with the help of offset.

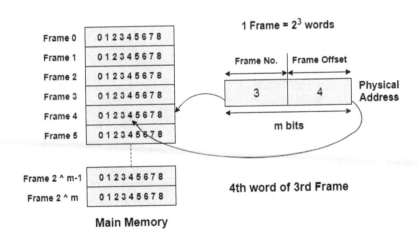

Main Memory

Mapping from page table to main memory

In operating systems, there is always a requirement of mapping from logical address to the physical address. However, this process involves various steps which are defined as follows.

1. Generation of logical address

CPU generates logical address for each page of the process. This contains two parts: page number and offset.

2. Scaling

To determine the actual page number of the process, CPU stores the page table base in a special register. Each time the address is generated, the value of the page table base is added to the page number to get the actual location of the page entry in the table. This process is called scaling.

3. Generation of physical Address

The frame number of the desired page is determined by its entry in the page table. A physical address is generated which also contains two parts: frame number and offset. The Offset will be similar to the offset of the logical address therefore it will be copied from the logical address.

4. Getting Actual Frame Number

The frame number and the offset from the physical address is mapped to the main memory in order to get the actual word address.

Page Table Entry

Along with page frame number, the page table also contains some of the bits representing the extra information regarding the page. Let's see what the each bit represents about the page.

1. Caching Disabled

Sometimes, there are differences between the information closest to the CPU and the information closest to the user. Operating system always wants CPU to access user's data as soon as possible. CPU accesses cache which can be inaccurate in some of the cases, therefore, OS can disable the cache for the required pages. This bit is set to 1 if the cache is disabled.

2. Referenced

There are various page replacement algorithms which will be covered later in this tutorial. This bit is set to 1 if the page is referred in the last clock cycle otherwise it remains 0.

3. Modified

This bit will be set if the page has been modified otherwise it remains 0.

4. Protection

The protection field represents the protection level which is applied on the page. It can be read only or read & write or execute. We need to remember that it is not a bit rather it is a field which contains many bits.

5. Present/Absent

In the concept of demand paging, all the pages doesn't need to be present in the main memory Therefore, for all the pages that are present in the main memory, this bit will be set to 1 and the bit will be 0 for all the pages which are absent.
If some page is not present in the main memory then it is called page fault.

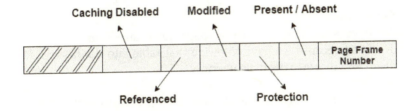

Size of the page table

However, the part of the process which is being executed by the CPU must be present in the main memory during that time period. The page table must also be present in the main memory all the time because it has the entry for all the pages.

The size of the page table depends upon the number of entries in the table and the bytes stored in one entry.

Let's consider,
Logical Address = 24 bits
Logical Address space = 2^{24} bytes
Let's say, Page size = 4 KB = 2^{12} Bytes

Page offset = 12

Number of bits in a page = Logical Address - Page Offset

= 24 - 12 = 12bits

Number of pages = 2^{12} = 2 X 2 X 10^{10} = 4 KB

Let's say, Page table entry = 1 Byte

Therefore, the size of the page table = 4 KB X 1 Byte = 4 KB

Here we are lucky enough to get the page table size equal to the frame size. Now, the page table will be simply stored in one of the frames of the main memory. The CPU maintains a register which contains the base address of that frame, every page number from the logical address will first be added to that base address so that we can access the actual location of the word being asked.

However, in some cases, the page table size and the frame size might not be same. In those cases, the page table is considered as the collection of frames and will be stored in the different frames.

Finding Optimal Page Size

We have seen that the bigger page table size cause an extra overhead because we have to divide that table into the pages and then store that into the main memory.

Our concern must be about executing processes not on the execution of page table. Page table provides a support for the execution of the process. The larger the page Table, the higher the overhead.

We know that,

Page Table Size = number of page entries in page table X size of one page entry

Let's consider an example,

Virtual Address Space = 2 GB = 2 X 2^{30} Bytes

Page Size = 2 KB = 2 X 2^{10} Bytes

Number of Pages in Page Table = (2 X 2^{30})/(2 X 2^{10}) = 1 M pages

There will be 1 million pages which is quite big number. However, try to make page size larger, say 2 MB.

Then, Number of pages in page table = $(2 \times 2^{30})/(2 \times 2^{20})$ = 1 K pages. If we compare the two scenarios, we can find out that the page table size is anti-proportional to Page Size.

In Paging, there is always wastage on the last page. If the virtual address space is not a multiple of page size, then there will be some bytes remaining and we have to assign a full page to those many bytes. This is simply an overhead.

Let's consider,
Page Size = 2 KB
Virtual Address Space = 17 KB
Then number of pages = 17 KB / 2 KB
The number of pages will be 9 although the 9th page will only contain 1 byte and the remaining page will be wasted.

In general,
If page size = p bytes
Entry size = e bytes
Virtual Address Space = S bytes
Then, overhead O = $(S/p) \times e + (p/2)$

On an average, the wasted number of pages in a virtual space is p/2(the half of total number of pages).

For, the minimal overhead,
$\partial O/\partial p = 0$
$-S/(p^2) + \frac{1}{2} = 0$
$p = \sqrt{(2.S.e)}$ bytes

Hence, if the page size $\sqrt{(2.S.e)}$ bytes then the overhead will be minimal.

Virtual Memory

Virtual Memory is a storage scheme that provides user an illusion of having a very big main memory. This is done by treating a part of secondary memory as the main memory.

In this scheme, User can load the bigger size processes than the available main memory by having the illusion that the memory is available to load the process.

Instead of loading one big process in the main memory, the Operating System loads the different parts of more than one process in the main memory.

By doing this, the degree of multiprogramming will be increased and therefore, the CPU utilization will also be increased.

How Virtual Memory Works?

In modern word, virtual memory has become quite common these days. In this scheme, whenever some pages needs to be loaded in the main memory for the execution and the memory is not available for those many pages, then in that case, instead of stopping the pages from entering in the main memory, the OS search for the RAM area that are least used in the recent times or that are not referenced and copy that into the secondary memory to make the space for the new pages in the main memory.

Since all this procedure happens automatically, therefore it makes the computer feel like it is having the unlimited RAM.

Demand Paging

Demand Paging is a popular method of virtual memory management. In demand paging, the pages of a process which are least used, get stored in the secondary memory.

A page is copied to the main memory when its demand is made or page fault occurs. There are various page replacement algorithms which are used to determine the pages which will be replaced. We will discuss each one of them later in detail.

Snapshot of a virtual memory management system

Let us assume 2 processes, P1 and P2, contains 4 pages each. Each page size is 1 KB. The main memory contains 8 frame of 1 KB each. The OS resides in the first two partitions. In the third partition,

1st page of P1 is stored and the other frames are also shown as filled with the different pages of processes in the main memory.

The page tables of both the pages are 1 KB size each and therefore they can be fit in one frame each. The page tables of both the processes contain various information that is also shown in the image.

The CPU contains a register which contains the base address of page table that is 5 in the case of P1 and 7 in the case of P2. This page table base address will be added to the page number of the Logical address when it comes to accessing the actual corresponding entry.

Frame	Present/ Absent	D Bit	Reference bit	Protection
0	0	0	0	
1	2	1	0	1
2	3	1	1	0
3	0	0	0	

Page Table of P1

Frame	Present/ Absent	D Bit	Reference bit	Protection
0	4	1	0	1
1		0	0	0
2		0	0	0
3		0	0	0

Page Table of P2

Main Memory:

0	
1	
2	P1 p1
3	P1 p2
4	P2 p0
5	Page Table of P1
6	
7	Page Table of P2

OS

Secondary Memory

P1: 0, 1, 2, 3
P2: 0, 1, 2, 3

CPU

5		7

Page Table Base (P1)   Page Table Base (P2)

Advantages of Virtual Memory

1. The degree of Multiprogramming will be increased.
2. User can run large application with less real RAM.
3. There is no need to buy more memory RAMs.

Disadvantages of Virtual Memory

1. The system becomes slower since swapping takes time.
2. It takes more time in switching between applications.
3. The user will have the lesser hard disk space for its use.

Drawbacks of Paging

1. Size of Page table can be very big and therefore it wastes main memory.

2. CPU will take more time to read a single word from the main memory.

How to decrease the page table size

1. The page table size can be decreased by increasing the page size but it will cause internal fragmentation and there will also be page wastage.

2. Other way is to use multilevel paging but that increases the effective access time therefore this is not a practical approach.

How to decrease the effective access time

1. CPU can use a register having the page table stored inside it so that the access time to access page table can become quite less but the register are not cheaper and they are very small in compare to the page table size therefore, this is also not a practical approach.

2. To overcome these many drawbacks in paging, we have to look for a memory that is cheaper than the register and faster than the main memory so that the time taken by the CPU to access page table again and again can be reduced and it can only focus to access the actual word.

Locality of reference

In operating systems, the concept of locality of reference states that, instead of loading the entire process in the main memory, OS can load only those number of pages in the main memory that are frequently accessed by the CPU and along with that, the OS can also load only those page table entries which are corresponding to those many pages.

Translation look aside buffer (TLB)

A Translation look aside buffer can be defined as a memory cache which can be used to reduce the time taken to access the page table again and again.

It is a memory cache which is closer to the CPU and the time taken by CPU to access TLB is lesser then that taken to access main memory.
In other words, we can say that TLB is faster and smaller than the main memory but cheaper and bigger than the register.
TLB follows the concept of locality of reference which means that it contains only the entries of those many pages that are frequently accessed by the CPU.

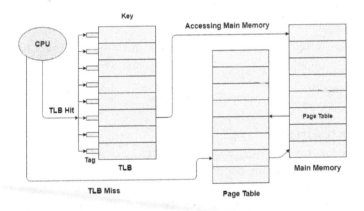

In translation look aside buffers, there are tags and keys with the help of which, the mapping is done.

TLB hit is a condition where the desired entry is found in translation look aside buffer. If this happens then the CPU simply access the actual location in the main memory.

However, if the entry is not found in TLB (TLB miss) then CPU has to access page table in the main memory and then access the actual frame in the main memory.

Therefore, in the case of TLB hit, the effective access time will be lesser as compare to the case of TLB miss.
If the probability of TLB hit is P% (TLB hit rate) then the probability of TLB miss (TLB miss rate) will be (1-P) %.

Therefore, the effective access time can be defined as;

$$EAT = P(t + m) + (1 - p)(t + k.m + m)$$

Where, p → TLB hit rate, t → time taken to access TLB, m → time taken to access main memory k = 1, if the single level paging has been implemented.

By the formula, we come to know that

1. Effective access time will be decreased if the TLB hit rate is increased.

2. Effective access time will be increased in the case of multilevel paging.

GATE Question on TLB

GATE | GATE-CS-2014-(Set-3)
Consider a paging hardware with a TLB. Assume that the entire page table and all the pages are in the physical memory. It takes 10 milliseconds to search the TLB and 80 milliseconds to access the physical memory. If the TLB hit ratio is 0.6, the effective memory access time (in milliseconds) is _____.
Given,

1. TLB hit ratio = 0.6

2. Therefore, TLB miss ratio = 0.4

3. Time taken to access TLB (t) = 10 ms

4. Time taken to access main memory (m) = 80 ms

Effective Access Time (EAT) = 0.6 (10 + 80) + 0.4 (10 + 80 + 80)

= 90 X 0.6 + 0.4 X 170 = 122

Demand Paging

According to the concept of Virtual Memory, in order to execute some process, only a part of the process needs to be present in the main memory which means that only a few pages will only be present in the main memory at any time.

However, deciding which pages need to be kept in the main memory and which need to be kept in the secondary memory, is difficult because we cannot say in advance that a process will require a particular page at a particular time.

Therefore, to overcome this problem, there is a concept called Demand Paging is introduced. It suggests keeping all pages of the frames in the secondary memory until they are required. In other words, it says that do not load any page in the main memory until it is required.

Whenever any page is referred for the first time in the main memory, then that page will be found in the secondary memory.
After that, it may or may not be present in the main memory depending upon the page replacement algorithm which will be covered later in this tutorial.

Page Fault

If the referred page is not present in the main memory then there will be a miss and the concept is called Page miss or page fault.

The CPU has to access the missed page from the secondary memory. If the number of page fault is very high then the effective access time of the system will become very high.

Thrashing

If the number of page faults is equal to the number of referred pages or the number of page faults are so high so that the CPU remains busy in just reading the pages from the secondary memory then the effective access time will be the time taken by the CPU to read one word from the secondary memory and it will be so high. The concept is called thrashing.

If the page fault rate is PF %, the time taken in getting a page from the secondary memory and again restarting is S (service time) and the memory access time is ma then the effective access time can be given as;

$$EAT = PF \times S + (1 - PF) \times (ma)$$

Inverted Page Table

Inverted Page Table is the global page table which is maintained by the Operating System for all the processes. In inverted page table, the number of entries is equal to the number of frames in the main memory. It can be used to overcome the drawbacks of page table. There is always a space reserved for the page regardless of the fact that whether it is present in the main memory or not. However, this is simply the wastage of the memory if the page is not present.

Pages	Frames		Pages	Frames
0	X		0	F2
1	X		1	F4
2	F1		2	F7
3	F3		3	X
4	F6		4	X
5	X		5	X
6	F5		6	F0

Page Table of P1   Page Table of P2

We can save this wastage by just inverting the page table. We can save the details only for the pages which are present in the main memory. Frames are the indices and the information saved inside the block will be Process ID and page number.

Pages	Frames
0	OS
1	P1 p2
2	P2 p0
3	P1 p3
4	P2 p1
5	P1 p6
6	P1 p4
7	P2 p2

Inverted Page Table

Page Replacement Algorithms

The page replacement algorithm decides which memory page is to be replaced. The process of replacement is sometimes called swap out or write to disk. Page replacement is done when the requested page is not found in the main memory (page fault).

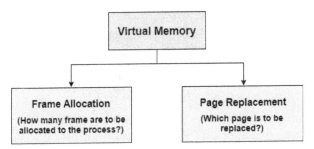

There are two main aspects of virtual memory, Frame allocation and Page Replacement. It is very important to have the optimal frame allocation and page replacement algorithm. Frame allocation is all about how many frames are to be allocated to the process while the page replacement is all about determining the page number which needs to be replaced in order to make space for the requested page.

What If the algorithm is not optimal?
1. If the number of frames which are allocated to a process is not sufficient or accurate then there can be a problem of thrashing. Due

to the lack of frames, most of the pages will be residing in the main memory and therefore more page faults will occur.

However, if OS allocates more frames to the process then there can be internal fragmentation.

2. If the page replacement algorithm is not optimal then there will also be the problem of thrashing. If the number of pages that are replaced by the requested pages will be referred in the near future then there will be more number of swap-in and swap-out and therefore the OS has to perform more replacements then usual which causes performance deficiency.

Therefore, the task of an optimal page replacement algorithm is to choose the page which can limit the thrashing.

Types of Page Replacement Algorithms

There are various page replacement algorithms. Each algorithm has a different method by which the pages can be replaced.

1. **Optimal Page Replacement algorithm:** this algorithms replaces the page which will not be referred for so long in future. Although it cannot be practically implementable but it can be used as a benchmark. Other algorithms are compared to this in terms of optimality.

2. **Least recent used (LRU) page replacement algorithm:** this algorithm replaces the page which has not been referred for a long time. This algorithm is just opposite to the optimal page replacement algorithm. In this, we look at the past instead of staring at future.

3. **FIFO:** in this algorithm, a queue is maintained. The page which is assigned the frame first will be replaced first. In other words, the page which resides at the rare end of the queue will be replaced on the every page fault.

GATE 2015 question on LRU and FIFO

Consider a main memory with five page frames and the following sequence of page references: 3, 8, 2, 3, 9, 1, 6, 3, 8, 9, 3, 6, 2, 1, 3.

Which one of the following is true with respect to page replacement policies First-In-First-out (FIFO) and Least Recently Used (LRU)?
A. Both incur the same number of page faults
B. FIFO incurs 2 more page faults than LRU
C. LRU incurs 2 more page faults than FIFO
D. FIFO incurs 1 more page faults than LRU

Solution
Number of frames = 5

FIFO
According to FIFO, the page which first comes in the memory will first goes out.

Request	3	8	2	3	9	1	6	3	8	9	3	6	2	1	3
Frame 5						1	1	1	1	1	1	1	1	1	1
Frame 4					9	9	9	9	9	9	9	9	2	2	2
Frame 3			2	2	2	2	2	2	8	8	8	8	8	8	8
Frame 2		8	8	8	8	8	8	3	3	3	3	3	3	3	3
Frame 1	3	3	3	3	3	3	6	6	6	6	6	6	6	6	6
Miss/Hit	Miss	Miss	Miss	Hit	Miss	Miss	Miss	Miss	Miss	Hit	Hit	Hit	Miss	Hit	Hit

Number of Page Faults = 9
Number of hits = 6

LRU
According to LRU, the page which has not been requested for a long time will get replaced with the new one.

Request	3	8	2	3	9	1	6	3	8	9	3	6	2	1	3
Frame 5						1	1	1	1	1	1	1	2	2	2
Frame 4					9	9	9	9	9	9	9	9	9	9	9
Frame 3			2	2	2	2	2	2	8	8	8	8	8	1	1
Frame 2		8	8	8	8	8	6	6	6	6	6	6	6	6	6
Frame 1	3	3	3	3	3	3	3	3	3	3	3	3	3	3	3
Miss/Hit	Miss	Miss	Miss	Hit	Miss	Miss	Hit	Hit	Miss	Hit	Miss	Hit	Miss	Miss	Hit

Number of Page Faults = 9
Number of Hits = 6
The Number of page faults in both the cases is equal therefore the Answer is option (A).

Numerical on Optimal, LRU and FIFO

Consider a reference string: 4, 7, 6, 1, 7, 6, 1, 2, 7, 2. the number of frames in the memory is 3. Find out the number of page faults respective to:

1. Optimal Page Replacement Algorithm
2. FIFO Page Replacement Algorithm
3. LRU Page Replacement Algorithm

Optimal Page Replacement Algorithm

Request	4	7	6	1	7	6	1	2	7	2
Frame 3			6	6	6	6	6	2	2	2
Frame 2		7	7	7	7	7	7	7	7	7
Frame 1	4	4	4	1	1	1	1	1	1	1
Miss/Hit	Miss	Miss	Miss	Miss	Hit	Hit	Hit	Miss	Hit	Hit

Number of Page Faults in Optimal Page Replacement Algorithm = 5

LRU Page Replacement Algorithm

Request	4	7	6	1	7	6	1	2	7	2
Frame 3			6	6	6	6	6	6	7	7
Frame 2		7	7	7	7	7	7	2	2	2
Frame 1	4	4	4	1	1	1	1	1	1	1
Miss/Hit	Miss	Miss	Miss	Miss	Hit	Hit	Hit	Miss	Miss	Hit

Number of Page Faults in LRU = 6

FIFO Page Replacement Algorithm

Request	4	7	6	1	7	6	1	2	7	2
Frame 3			6	6	6	6	6	6	7	7
Frame 2		7	7	7	7	7	7	2	2	2
Frame 1	4	4	4	1	1	1	1	1	1	1
Miss/Hit	Miss	Miss	Miss	Miss	Hit	Hit	Hit	Miss	Miss	Hit

Number of Page Faults in FIFO = 6

Belady's Anomaly

In the case of LRU and optimal page replacement algorithms, it is seen that the number of page faults will be reduced if we increase the number of frames. However, Belady found that, In FIFO page replacement algorithm, the number of page faults will get increased with the increment in number of frames.

This is the strange behavior shown by FIFO algorithm in some of the cases. This is an Anomaly called as Belady's Anomaly.

Let's examine such an example:
The reference String is given as 0 1 5 3 0 1 4 0 1 5 3 4. Let's analyze the behavior of FIFO algorithm in two cases.

Case 1: Number of frames = 3

Request	0	1	5	3	0	1	4	0	1	5	3	4
Frame 3			5	5	5	1	1	1	1	1	3	3
Frame 2		1	1	1	0	0	0	0	0	5	5	5
Frame 1	0	0	0	3	3	3	4	4	4	4	4	4
Miss/Hit	Miss	Miss	Miss	Miss	Miss	Miss	Miss	Hit	Hit	Miss	Miss	Hit

Number of Page Faults = 9

Case 2: Number of frames = 4

Request	0	1	5	3	0	1	4	0	1	5	3	4
Frame 4				3	3	3	3	3	3	5	5	5
Frame 3			5	5	5	5	5	5	1	1	1	1
Frame 2		1	1	1	1	1	1	0	0	0	0	4
Frame 1	0	0	0	0	0	0	4	4	4	4	3	3
Miss/Hit	Miss	Miss	Miss	Miss	Hit	Hit	Miss	Miss	Miss	Miss	Miss	Miss

Number of Page Faults = 10

Therefore, in this example, the number of page faults is increasing by increasing the number of frames hence this suffers from Belady's Anomaly.

Segmentation

In Operating Systems, Segmentation is a memory management technique in which, the memory is divided into the variable size parts. Each part is known as segment which can be allocated to a process.

The details about each segment are stored in a table called as segment table. Segment table is stored in one (or many) of the segments.

Segment table contains mainly two information about segment:

1. Base: It is the base address of the segment
2. Limit: It is the length of the segment.

Why Segmentation is required?

Till now, we were using Paging as our main memory management technique. Paging is more close to Operating system rather than the User. It divides all the process into the form of pages regardless of the fact that a process can have some relative parts of functions which needs to be loaded in the same page.

Operating system doesn't care about the User's view of the process. It may divide the same function into different pages and those pages may or may not be loaded at the same time into the memory. It decreases the efficiency of the system.

It is better to have segmentation which divides the process into the segments. Each segment contain same type of functions such as main function can be included in one segment and the library functions can be included in the other segment.

Translation of Logical address into physical address by segment table

CPU generates a logical address which contains two parts:

1. Segment Number
2. Offset

The Segment number is mapped to the segment table. The limit of the respective segment is compared with the offset. If the offset is less than the limit then the address is valid otherwise it throws an error as the address is invalid.

In the case of valid address, the base address of the segment is added to the offset to get the physical address of actual word in the main memory.

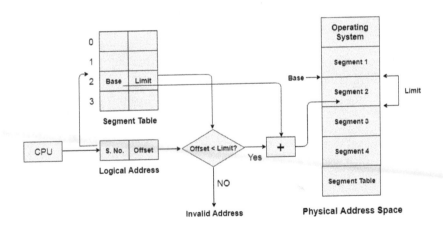

Advantages of Segmentation

1. No internal fragmentation
2. Average Segment Size is larger than the actual page size.
3. Less overhead
4. It is easier to relocate segments than entire address space.
5. The segment table is of lesser size as compare to the page table in paging.

Disadvantages of Segmentation

1. It can have external fragmentation.
2. it is difficult to allocate contiguous memory to variable sized partition.
3. Costly memory management algorithms.

Paging vs Segmentation

Paging	Segmentation
Non-Contiguous memory allocation	Non-contiguous memory allocation
Paging divides program into fixed size pages.	Segmentation divides program into variable size segments.
OS is responsible	Compiler is responsible.
Paging is faster than segmentation	Segmentation is slower than paging
Paging is closer to Operating System	Segmentation is closer to User
It suffers from internal fragmentation	It suffers from external fragmentation
There is no external fragmentation	There is no external fragmentation
Logical address is divided into page number and page offset	Logical address is divided into segment number and segment offset
Page table is used to maintain the page information.	Segment Table maintains the segment information
Page table entry has the frame number and some flag bits to represent details about pages.	Segment table entry has the base address of the segment and some protection bits for the segments.

Segmented Paging

Pure segmentation is not very popular and not being used in many of the operating systems. However, Segmentation can be combined with Paging to get the best features out of both the techniques.
In Segmented Paging, the main memory is divided into variable size segments which are further divided into fixed size pages.

1. Pages are smaller than segments.
2. Each Segment has a page table which means every program has multiple page tables.
3. The logical address is represented as Segment Number (base address), Page number and page offset.

Segment Number: It points to the appropriate Segment Number.
Page Number: It Points to the exact page within the segment

Page Offset: Used as an offset within the page frame

Each Page table contains the various information about every page of the segment. The Segment Table contains the information about every segment. Each segment table entry points to a page table entry and every page table entry is mapped to one of the page within a segment.

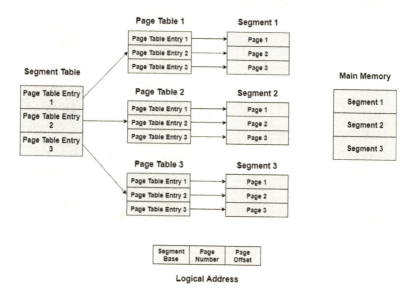

Translation of logical address to physical address

The CPU generates a logical address which is divided into two parts: Segment Number and Segment Offset. The Segment Offset must be less than the segment limit. Offset is further divided into Page number and Page Offset. To map the exact page number in the page table, the page number is added into the page table base.

The actual frame number with the page offset is mapped to the main memory to get the desired word in the page of the certain segment of the process.

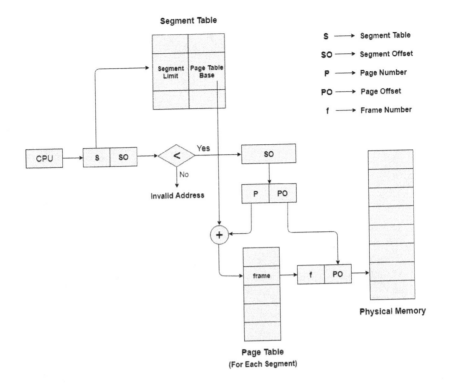

Advantages of Segmented Paging

1. It reduces memory usage.
2. Page table size is limited by the segment size.
3. Segment table has only one entry corresponding to one actual segment.
4. External Fragmentation is not there.
5. It simplifies memory allocation.

Disadvantages of Segmented Paging

1. Internal Fragmentation will be there.
2. The complexity level will be much higher as compare to paging.
3. Page Tables need to be contiguously stored in the memory.

Chapter 7 – File Management

A **file** can be defined as a data structure which stores the sequence of records. Files are stored in a file system, which may exist on a disk or in the main memory. Files can be simple (plain text) or complex (specially-formatted).

The collection of files is known as Directory. The collection of directories at the different levels, is known as a **File System**.

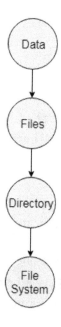

Attributes of the File

1. Name
Every file carries a name by which the file is recognized in the file system. One directory cannot have two files with the same name.

2. Identifier
Along with the name, each file has its own extension which identifies the type of the file. For example, a text file has the extension .txt, a video file can have the extension .mp4.

3. Type
In a File System, the Files are classified in different types such as video files, audio files, text files, executable files, etc.

4. Location
In the File System, there are several locations on which, the files can be stored. Each file carries its location as its attribute.

5. Size
The Size of the File is one of its most important attribute. By size of the file, we mean the number of bytes acquired by the file in the memory.

6. Protection
The Admin of the computer may want the different protections for the different files. Therefore each file carries its own set of permissions to the different group of Users.

7. Time and Date
Every file carries a time stamp which contains the time and date on which the file is last modified.

Operations on the File

There are various operations which can be implemented on a file. We will see all of them in detail.

1. Create

Creation of the file is the most important operation on the file. Different types of files are created by different methods for example text editors are used to create a text file, word processors are used to create a word file and Image editors are used to create the image files.

2. Write

Writing the file is different from creating the file. The OS maintains a write pointer for every file which points to the position in the file from which, the data needs to be written.

3. Read

Every file is opened in three different modes: Read, Write and append. A Read pointer is maintained by the OS, pointing to the position up to which, the data has been read.

4. Re-position

Re-positioning is simply moving the file pointers forward or backward depending upon the user's requirement. It is also called as seeking.

5. Delete

Deleting the file will not only delete all the data stored inside the file, it also deletes all the attributes of the file. The space which is allocated to the file will now become available and can be allocated to the other files.

6. Truncate

Truncating is simply deleting the file except deleting attributes. The file is not completely deleted although the information stored inside the file get replaced.

File Access Methods

Let's look at various ways to access files stored in secondary memory.

1. Sequential Access

Most of the operating systems access the file sequentially. In other words, we can say that most of the files need to be accessed sequentially by the operating system.

In sequential access, the OS read the file word by word. A pointer is maintained which initially points to the base address of the file. If the user wants to read first word of the file then the pointer provides that word to the user and increases its value by 1 word. This process continues till the end of the file.

Modern word systems do provide the concept of direct access and indexed access but the most used method is sequential access due to the fact that most of the files such as text files, audio files, video files, etc. need to be sequentially accessed.

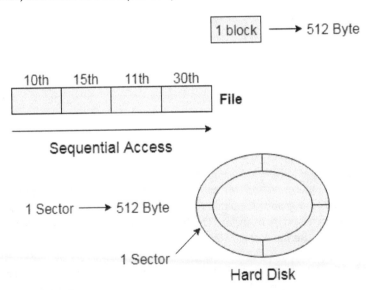

2. Direct Access

The **Direct Access** is mostly required in the case of database systems. In most of the cases, we need filtered information from the database. The sequential access can be very slow and inefficient in such cases.

Suppose every block of the storage stores 4 records and we know that the record we needed is stored in 10th block. In that case, the sequential access will not be implemented because it will traverse all the blocks in order to access the needed record.

Direct access will give the required result despite of the fact that the operating system has to perform some complex tasks such as determining the desired block number. However, that is generally implemented in database applications.

Sequential Access

Direct Access

Database System

3. Indexed Access

If a file can be sorted on any of the filed then an index can be assigned to a group of certain records. However, a particular record can be accessed by its index. The index is nothing but the address of a record in the file.

In index accessing, searching in a large database became very quick and easy but we need to have some extra space in the memory to store the index value.

Directory Structure

A **Directory** can be defined as the listing of the related files on the disk. The directory may store some or the entire file attributes.

To get the benefit of different file systems on the different operating systems, a hard disk can be divided into the number of partitions of different sizes. The partitions are also called volumes or mini disks.

Each partition must have at least one directory in which, all the files of the partition can be listed. A directory entry is maintained for each file in the directory which stores all the information related to that file.

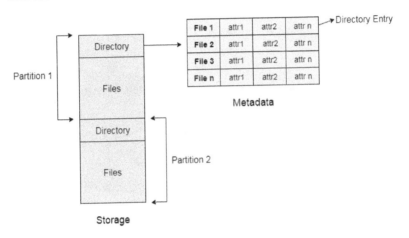

A directory can be viewed as a file which contains the Meta data of the bunch of files.

Every Directory supports a number of common operations on the file:

1. File Creation
2. Search for the file
3. File deletion
4. Renaming the file
5. Traversing Files
6. Listing of files

Single Level Directory

The simplest method is to have one big list of all the files on the disk. The entire system will contain only one directory which is supposed to mention all the files present in the file system. The directory contains one entry per each file present on the file system.

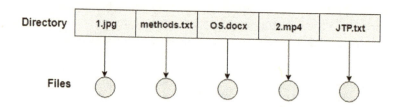

This type of directories can be used for a simple system.

Advantages

1. Implementation is very simple.
2. If the sizes of the files are very small then the searching becomes faster.
3. File creation, searching, deletion is very simple since we have only one directory.

Disadvantages

1. We cannot have two files with the same name.
2. The directory may be very big therefore searching for a file may take so much time.
3. Protection cannot be implemented for multiple users.
4. There are no ways to group same kind of files.
5. Choosing the unique name for every file is a bit complex and limits the number of files in the system because most of the Operating System limits the number of characters used to construct the file name.

Two Level Directory

In two level directory systems, we can create a separate directory for each user. There is one master directory which contains separate directories dedicated to each user. For each user, there is a different directory present at the second level, containing group of user's file. The system doesn't let a user to enter in the other user's directory without permission.

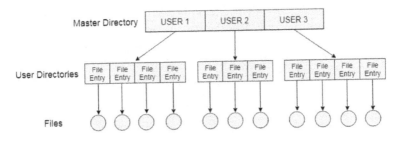

Characteristics of two level directory system

1. Each files has a path name as /User-name/directory-name/
2. Different users can have the same file name.
3. Searching becomes more efficient as only one user's list needs to be traversed.
4. The same kind of files cannot be grouped into a single directory for a particular user.

Every Operating System maintains a variable as PWD which contains the present directory name (present user name) so that the searching can be done appropriately.

Tree Structured Directory

In the Tree structured directory system, any directory entry can either be a file or sub directory. Tree structured directory system overcomes the drawbacks of two level directory system. The similar kind of files can now be grouped in one directory.

Each user has its own directory and it cannot enter in the other user's directory. However, the user has the permission to read the root's data but he cannot write or modify this. Only administrator of the system has the complete access of root directory.

Searching is more efficient in this directory structure. The concept of current working directory is used. A file can be accessed by two types of path, either relative or absolute.

Absolute path is the path of the file with respect to the root directory of the system while relative path is the path with respect to the current working directory of the system. In tree structured directory systems, the user is given the privilege to create the files as well as directories.

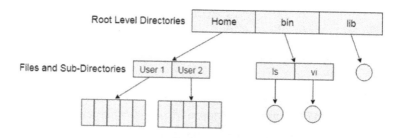

Permissions on the file and directory

A tree structured directory system may consist of various levels therefore there is a set of permissions assigned to each file and directory.

The permissions are **R W X** which are regarding reading, writing and the execution of the files or directory. The permissions are assigned to three types of users: owner, group and others.

There is an identification bit which differentiate between directory and file. For a directory, it is **d** and for a file, it is dot (.)

The following snapshot shows the permissions assigned to a file in a Linux based system. Initial bit **d** represents that it is a directory.

```
                              robertkaramagi@oel7:~                    _  □  ×
 File  Edit  View  Search  Terminal  Help
[robertkaramagi@oel7 ~]$ ls -l
total 0
drwxr-xr-x. 2 robertkaramagi robertkaramagi  6 May 21 04:32 Desktop
drwxr-xr-x. 4 robertkaramagi robertkaramagi 42 May 21 05:22 Documents
drwxr-xr-x. 2 robertkaramagi robertkaramagi  6 May 21 04:32 Downloads
drwxr-xr-x. 2 robertkaramagi robertkaramagi  6 May 21 04:32 Music
drwxr-xr-x. 2 robertkaramagi robertkaramagi  6 May 21 04:47 oraInventory
drwxr-xr-x. 2 robertkaramagi robertkaramagi  6 May 21 04:32 Pictures
drwxr-xr-x. 2 robertkaramagi robertkaramagi  6 May 21 04:32 Public
drwxr-xr-x. 2 robertkaramagi robertkaramagi  6 May 21 04:32 Templates
drwxr-xr-x. 2 robertkaramagi robertkaramagi  6 May 21 04:32 Videos
[robertkaramagi@oel7 ~]$ █
```

Acyclic-Graph Structured Directories

The tree structured directory system doesn't allow the same file to exist in multiple directories therefore sharing is major concern in tree structured directory system. We can provide sharing by making the directory an acyclic graph. In this system, two or more directory entry can point to the same file or sub directory. That file or sub directory is shared between the two directory entries.

These kinds of directory graphs can be made using links or aliases. We can have multiple paths for a same file. Links can either be symbolic (logical) or hard link (physical).

If a file gets deleted in acyclic graph structured directory system, then
1. In the case of soft link, the file just gets deleted and we are left with a dangling pointer.
2. In the case of hard link, the actual file will be deleted only if all the references to it gets deleted.

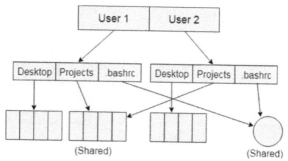

(Shared)   (Shared)

File Systems

File system is the part of the operating system which is responsible for file management. It provides a mechanism to store the data and access to the file contents including data and programs. Some Operating systems treats everything as a file for example Ubuntu. The File system takes care of the following issues:

- **File Structure**
  We have seen various data structures in which the file can be stored. The task of the file system is to maintain an optimal file structure.

- **Recovering Free space**
  Whenever a file gets deleted from the hard disk, there is a free space created in the disk. There can be many such spaces which need to be recovered in order to reallocate them to other files.

- **Disk space assignment to the files**
  The major concern about the file is deciding where to store the files on the hard disk. There are various disks scheduling algorithm which will be covered later in this tutorial.

- **Tracking data location**
  A File may or may not be stored within only one block. It can be stored in the non-contiguous blocks on the disk. We need to keep track of all the blocks on which the part of the files reside.

File System Structure

File Systems provide efficient access to the disk by allowing data to be stored, located and retrieved in a convenient way. A file System must be able to store the file, locate the file and retrieve the file.

Most of the Operating Systems use layering approach for every task including file systems. Every layer of the file system is responsible for some activities.

The image shown below, elaborates how the file system is divided in different layers, and also the functionality of each layer.

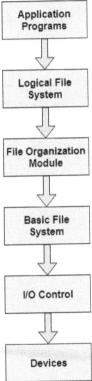

- When an application program asks for a file, the first request is directed to the logical file system. The logical file system contains the Meta data of the file and directory structure. If the application program doesn't have the required permissions of the file then this layer will throw an error. Logical file systems also verify the path to the file.

- Generally, files are divided into various logical blocks. Files are to be stored in the hard disk and to be retrieved from the hard disk. Hard disk is divided into various tracks and sectors. Therefore, in order to store and retrieve the files, the logical blocks need to be mapped to physical blocks. This mapping is done by File organization module. It is also responsible for free space management.

- Once File organization module decided which physical block the application program needs, it passes this information to basic file system. The basic file system is responsible for issuing the commands to I/O control in order to fetch those blocks.

- I/O controls contain the codes by using which it can access hard disk. These codes are known as device drivers. I/O controls are also responsible for handling interrupts.

Master Boot Record (MBR)

Master boot record is the information present in the first sector of any hard disk. It contains the information regarding how and where the Operating system is located in the hard disk so that it can be booted in the RAM.

MBR is sometimes called master partition table because it includes a partition table which locates every partition in the hard disk.

Master boot record (MBR) also includes a program which reads the boot sector record of the partition that contains operating system.

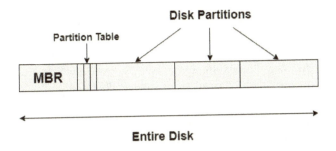

Disk Partitions

Partition Table

MBR

Entire Disk

What happens when you turn on your computer?

Due to the fact that the main memory is volatile, when we turn on our computer, CPU cannot access the main memory directly. However, there is a special program called as BIOS stored in ROM is accessed for the first time by the CPU.

BIOS contains the code, by executing which, the CPU access the very first partition of hard disk that is MBR. It contains a partition table for all the partitions of the hard disk.

Since, MBR contains the information about where the operating system is being stored and it also contains a program which can read the boot sector record of the partition, hence the CPU fetches all this information and load the operating system into the main memory.

On Disk Data Structures

There are various on disk data structures that are used to implement a file system. This structure may vary depending upon the operating system.

1. **Boot Control Block**

   Boot Control Block contains all the information which is needed to boot an operating system from that volume. It is called boot block in UNIX file system. In NTFS, it is called the partition boot sector.

2. **Volume Control Block**

   Volume control block all the information regarding that volume such as number of blocks, size of each block, partition table, pointers to free blocks and free FCB blocks. In UNIX file system, it is known as super block. In NTFS, this information is stored inside master file table.

3. **Directory Structure (per file system)**

   A directory structure (per file system) contains file names and pointers to corresponding FCBs. In UNIX, it includes inode numbers associated to file names.

4. **File Control Block**

   File Control block contains all the details about the file such as ownership details, permission details, file size, etc. In UFS, this detail is stored in inode. In NTFS, this information is stored inside master file table as a relational database structure. A typical file control block is shown in the image below.

| File Permissions |
| File Dates (Create, Access, Write) |
| File Owner, Group, ACL |
| File Size |
| File Data Blocks |

File Control Block

In Memory Data Structure

Till now, we have discussed the data structures that are required to be present on the hard disk in order to implement file systems.

Here, we will discuss the data structures required to be present in memory in order to implement the file system.

The in-memory data structures are used for file system management as well as performance improvement via caching. This information is loaded on the mount time and discarded on ejection.

1. **In-memory Mount Table**
    In-memory mount table contains the list of all the devices which are being mounted to the system. Whenever the connection is maintained to a device, its entry will be done in the mount table.

2. **In-memory Directory structure cache**
    This is the list of directory which is recently accessed by the CPU. The directories present in the list can also be accessed in the near future so it will be better to store them temporally in cache.

3. **System-wide open file table**
    This is the list of all the open files in the system at a particular time. Whenever the user open any file for reading or writing, the entry will be made in this open file table.

4. **Per process Open file table**
    It is the list of open files subjected to every process. Since there is already a list which is there for every open file in the system therefore it only contains Pointers to the appropriate entry in the system wide table.

Directory Implementation

There is the number of algorithms by using which, the directories can be implemented. However, the selection of an appropriate directory implementation algorithm may significantly affect the performance of the system.

The directory implementation algorithms are classified according to the data structure they are using. There are mainly two algorithms which are used in these days.

Linear List

In this algorithm, all the files in a directory are maintained as singly lined list. Each file contains the pointers to the data blocks which are assigned to it and the next file in the directory.

Characteristics

1. When a new file is created, then the entire list is checked whether the new file name is matching to an existing file name or not. In case, it doesn't exist, the file can be created at the beginning or at the end. Therefore, searching for a unique name is a big concern because traversing the whole list takes time.

2. The list needs to be traversed in case of every operation (creation, deletion, updating, etc.) on the files therefore the systems become inefficient.

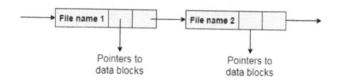

Hash Table

To overcome the drawbacks of singly linked list implementation of directories, there is an alternative approach that is hash table. This approach suggests to use hash table along with the linked lists.

A key-value pair for each file in the directory gets generated and stored in the hash table. The key can be determined by applying the hash function on the file name while the key points to the corresponding file stored in the directory.

Now, searching becomes efficient due to the fact that now, entire list will not be searched on every operating. Only hash table entries are checked using the key and if an entry found then the corresponding file will be fetched using the value.

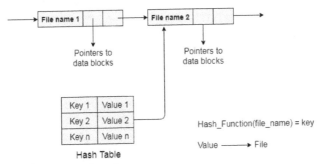

Allocation Methods

There are various methods which can be used to allocate disk space to the files. Selection of an appropriate allocation method will significantly affect the performance and efficiency of the system.

Allocation method provides a way in which the disk will be utilized and the files will be accessed. There are following methods which can be used for allocation.

1. Contiguous Allocation
2. Extents
3. Linked List Allocation
4. Clustering
5. File Allocation Table
6. Indexed Allocation
7. Linked Indexed Allocation
8. Multilevel Indexed Allocation
9. Inode

Contiguous Allocation

If the blocks are allocated to the file in such a way that all the logical blocks of the file get the contiguous physical block in the hard disk then such allocation scheme is known as contiguous allocation.

In the image shown below, there are three files in the directory. The starting block and the length of each file are mentioned in the table. We can check in the table that the contiguous blocks are assigned to each file as per its need.

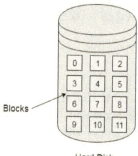

File Name	Start	Length	Allocated Blocks
abc.text	0	3	0,1,2
video.mp4	4	2	4,5
jtp.docx	9	3	9,10,11

Hard Disk   Directory

Advantages

1. It is simple to implement.
2. We will get Excellent read performance.
3. Supports Random Access into files.

Disadvantages

1. The disk will become fragmented.
2. It may be difficult to have a file grow.

Linked List Allocation

Linked List allocation solves all problems of contiguous allocation. In linked list allocation, each file is considered as the linked list of disk blocks. However, the disks blocks allocated to a particular file need not to be contiguous on the disk. Each disk block allocated to a file contains a pointer which points to the next disk block allocated to the same file.

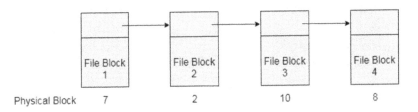

Advantages

1. There is no external fragmentation with linked allocation.
2. Any free block can be utilized in order to satisfy the file block requests.
3. File can continue to grow as long as the free blocks are available.
4. Directory entry will only contain the starting block address.

Disadvantages

1. Random Access is not provided.
2. Pointers require some space in the disk blocks.
3. Any of the pointers in the linked list must not be broken otherwise the file will get corrupted.
4. Need to traverse each block.

File Allocation Table

The main disadvantage of linked list allocation is that the Random access to a particular block is not provided. In order to access a block, we need to access all its previous blocks.

File Allocation Table overcomes this drawback of linked list allocation. In this scheme, a file allocation table is maintained, which gathers all the disk block links. The table has one entry for each disk block and is indexed by block number.

File allocation table needs to be cached in order to reduce the number of head seeks. Now the head doesn't need to traverse all the disk blocks in order to access one successive block.

It simply accesses the file allocation table, read the desired block entry from there and access that block. This is the way by which the random access is accomplished by using FAT. It is used by MS-DOS and pre-NT Windows versions.

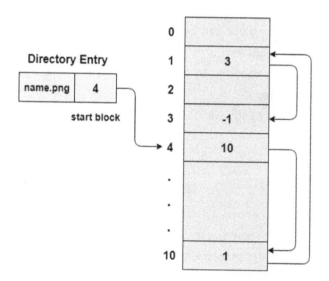

Advantages

1. Uses the whole disk block for data.
2. A bad disk block doesn't cause all successive blocks lost.
3. Random access is provided although it's not too fast.
4. Only FAT needs to be traversed in each file operation.

Disadvantages

1. Each Disk block needs a FAT entry.
2. FAT size may be very big depending upon the number of FAT entries.
3. Number of FAT entries can be reduced by increasing the block size but it will also increase Internal Fragmentation.

Limitation of FAT

Limitation in the existing technology causes the evolution of a new technology. Till now, we have seen various allocation methods; each of them was carrying several advantages and disadvantages.

File allocation table tries to solve as many problems as possible but leads to a drawback. The more the number of blocks, the more will be the size of FAT.

Therefore, we need to allocate more space to a file allocation table. Since, file allocation table needs to be cached therefore it is impossible to have as many space in cache. Here we need a new technology which can solve such problems.

Indexed Allocation

Instead of maintaining a file allocation table of all the disk pointers, Indexed allocation scheme stores all the disk pointers in one of the blocks called as indexed block. Indexed block doesn't hold the file data, but it holds the pointers to all the disk blocks allocated to that particular file. Directory entry will only contain the index block address.

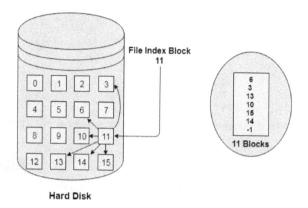

Hard Disk

Advantages

1. Supports direct access
2. A bad data block causes the loss of only that block.

Disadvantages

1. A bad index block could cause the loss of the entire file.
2. Size of a file depends upon the number of pointers, an index block can hold.
3. Having an index block for a small file is a waste.
4. More pointer overhead

Linked Index Allocation

In **Linked index allocation**, the file size depends on the size of a disk block. To allow large files, we have to link several index blocks together. In linked index allocation,

- Small header giving the name of the file
- Set of the first 100 block addresses
- Pointer to another index block

For the larger files, the last entry of the index block is a pointer which points to another index block. This is also called as linked schema.

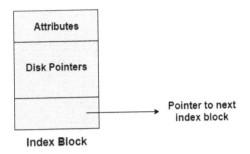

Index Block

Advantage: It removes file size limitations
Disadvantage: Random Access becomes a bit harder

Multilevel Index Allocation

In **Multilevel index allocation**, we have various levels of indices. There are outer level index blocks which contain the pointers to the inner level index blocks and the inner level index blocks contain the pointers to the file data.

- The outer level index is used to find the inner level index.
- The inner level index is used to find the desired data block.

Advantage: Random Access becomes better and efficient.
Disadvantage: Access time for a file will be higher.

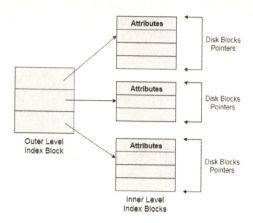

Outer Level
Index Block

Inner Level
Index Blocks

Inode

In UNIX based operating systems, each file is indexed by an Inode. Inode are the special disk block which is created with the creation of the file system. The number of files or directories in a file system depends on the number of Inodes in the file system.

An Inode includes the following information:

1. Attributes (permissions, time stamp, ownership details, etc.) of the file

2. A number of direct blocks which contains the pointers to first 12 blocks of the file.

3. A single indirect pointer which points to an index block. If the file cannot be indexed entirely by the direct blocks then the single indirect pointer is used.

4. A double indirect pointer which points to a disk block that is a collection of the pointers to the disk blocks which are index blocks. Double index pointer is used if the file is too big to be indexed entirely by the direct blocks as well as the single indirect pointer.

5. A triple index pointer that points to a disk block that is a collection of pointers. Each of the pointers is separately pointing to a disk block which also contains a collection of

pointers which are separately pointing to an index block that contains the pointers to the file blocks.

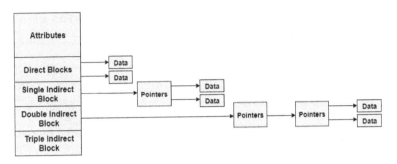

Free Space Management

A file system is responsible to allocate the free blocks to the file therefore it has to keep track of all the free blocks present in the disk. There are mainly two approaches by using which, the free blocks in the disk are managed.

1. Bit Vector

In this approach, the free space list is implemented as a bit map vector. It contains the number of bits where each bit represents each block.

If the block is empty then the bit is 1 otherwise it is 0. Initially all the blocks are empty therefore each bit in the bit map vector contains 1. LAs the space allocation proceeds, the file system starts allocating blocks to the files and setting the respective bit to 0.

2. Linked List

It is another approach for free space management. This approach suggests linking together all the free blocks and keeping a pointer in the cache which points to the first free block.

Therefore, all the free blocks on the disks will be linked together with a pointer. Whenever a block gets allocated, its previous free block will be linked to its next free block.

Disk Scheduling

As we know, a process needs two type of time, CPU time and IO time. For I/O, it requests the Operating system to access the disk.

However, the operating system must be fair enough to satisfy each request and at the same time, operating system must maintain the efficiency and speed of process execution.

The technique that operating system uses to determine the request which is to be satisfied next is called disk scheduling.

Let's discuss some important terms related to disk scheduling.

Seek Time

Seek time is the time taken in locating the disk arm to a specified track where the read/write request will be satisfied.

Rotational Latency

It is the time taken by the desired sector to rotate itself to the position from where it can access the R/W heads.

Transfer Time

It is the time taken to transfer the data.

Disk Access Time

Disk access time is given as,

Disk Access Time = Rotational Latency + Seek Time + Transfer Time

Disk Response Time

It is the average of time spent by each request waiting for the IO operation.

Purpose of Disk Scheduling

The main purpose of disk scheduling algorithm is to select a disk request from the queue of IO requests and decide the schedule when this request will be processed.

Advantage

- Fairness
- High throughout
- Minimal traveling head time

Disk Scheduling Algorithms

The list of various disks scheduling algorithm is given below. Each algorithm is carrying some advantages and disadvantages. The limitation of each algorithm leads to the evolution of a new algorithm.

- FCFS scheduling algorithm
- SSTF (shortest seek time first) algorithm
- SCAN scheduling
- C-SCAN scheduling
- LOOK Scheduling
- C-LOOK scheduling

FCFS Scheduling Algorithm

It is the simplest Disk Scheduling algorithm. It services the IO requests in the order in which they arrive. There is no starvation in this algorithm, every request is serviced.

Disadvantages

- The scheme does not optimize the seek time.

- The request may come from different processes therefore there is the possibility of inappropriate movement of the head.

Example

Consider the following disk request sequence for a disk with 100 tracks 45, 21, 67, 90, 4, 50, 89, 52, 61, 87, 25

Head pointer starting at 50 and moving in left direction. Find the number of head movements in cylinders using FCFS scheduling.

Solution

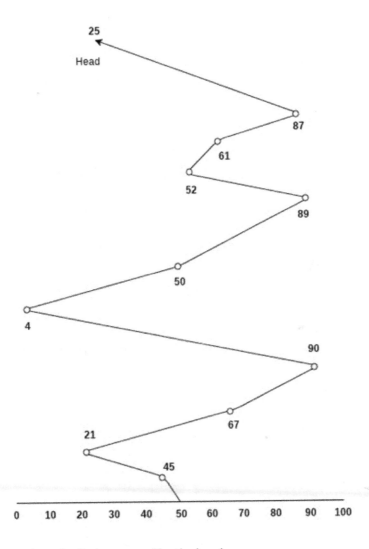

Number of cylinders moved by the head
=(50-45)+(45-21)+(67-21)+(90-67)+(90-4)+(50-4)+(89-50)+(61-52)+(87-61)+(87-25)
= 5 + 24 + 46 + 23 + 86 + 46 + 49 + 9 + 26 + 62
= 376

SSTF Scheduling Algorithm

Shortest seek time first (SSTF) algorithm selects the disk I/O request which requires the least disk arm movement from its current position regardless of the direction. It reduces the total seek time as compared to FCFS. It allows the head to move to the closest track in the service queue.

Disadvantages

- It may cause starvation for some requests.
- Switching direction on the frequent basis slows the working of algorithm.
- It is not the most optimal algorithm.

Example

Consider the following disk request sequence for a disk with 100 tracks

45, 21, 67, 90, 4, 89, 52, 61, 87, 25
Head pointer starting at 50. Find the number of head movements in cylinders using SSTF scheduling.

Solution:

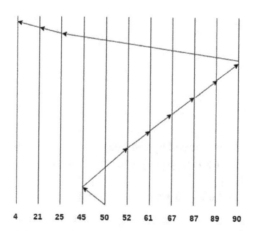

Number of cylinders = 5 + 7 + 9 + 6 + 20 + 2 + 1 + 65 + 4 + 17 = 136

SCAN and C-SCAN algorithm

SCAN

It is also called as **Elevator Algorithm**. In this algorithm, the disk arm moves into a particular direction till the end, satisfying all the requests coming in its path and then it turns back and moves in the reverse direction satisfying requests coming in its path.

It works in the way an elevator works, elevator moves in a direction completely till the last floor of that direction and then turns back.

Example

Consider the following disk request sequence for a disk with 100 tracks

98, 137, 122, 183, 14, 133, 65, 78

Head pointer starting at 54 and moving in left direction. Find the number of head movements in cylinders using SCAN scheduling.

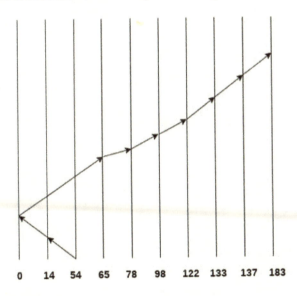

Number of Cylinders = 40 + 14 + 65 + 13 + 20 + 24 + 11 + 4 + 46 = 237

C-SCAN

In **C-SCAN algorithm**, the arm of the disk moves in a particular direction servicing requests until it reaches the last cylinder, then it jumps to the last cylinder of the opposite direction without servicing any request then it turns back and start moving in that direction servicing the remaining requests.

Example
Consider the following disk request sequence for a disk with 100 tracks
98, 137, 122, 183, 14, 133, 65, 78

Head pointer starting at 54 and moving in left direction. Find the number of head movements in cylinders using C-SCAN scheduling.

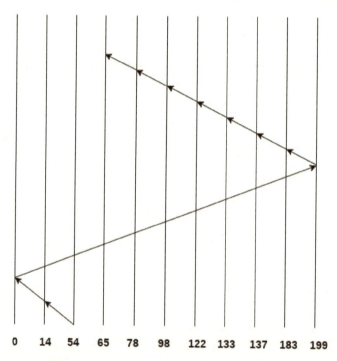

| 0 | 14 | 54 | 65 | 78 | 98 | 122 | 133 | 137 | 183 | 199 |

No. of cylinders crossed = 40 + 14 + 199 + 16 + 46 + 4 + 11 + 24 + 20 + 13 = 387

Look Scheduling

It is like SCAN scheduling Algorithm to some extant except the difference that, in this scheduling algorithm, the arm of the disk stops moving inwards (or outwards) when no more request in that direction exists. This algorithm tries to overcome the overhead of SCAN algorithm which forces disk arm to move in one direction till the end regardless of knowing if any request exists in the direction or not.

Example
Consider the following disk request sequence for a disk with 100 tracks
98, 137, 122, 183, 14, 133, 65, 78
Head pointer starting at 54 and moving in left direction. Find the number of head movements in cylinders using LOOK scheduling.

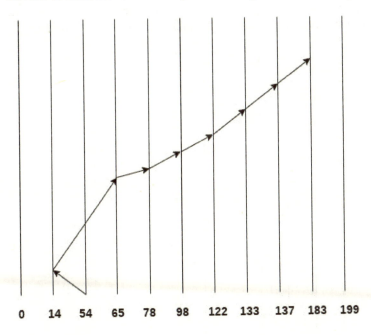

| 0 | 14 | 54 | 65 | 78 | 98 | 122 | 133 | 137 | 183 | 199 |

Number of cylinders crossed = 40 + 51 + 13 + +20 + 24 + 11 + 4 + 46 = 209

C Look Scheduling

C Look Algorithm is similar to C-SCAN algorithm to some extent. In this algorithm, the arm of the disk moves outwards servicing requests until it reaches the highest request cylinder, then it jumps to the lowest request cylinder without servicing any request then it again start moving outwards servicing the remaining requests.

It is different from C SCAN algorithm in the sense that, C SCAN force the disk arm to move till the last cylinder regardless of knowing whether any request is to be serviced on that cylinder or not.

Example

Consider the following disk request sequence for a disk with 100 tracks

98, 137, 122, 183, 14, 133, 65, 78

Head pointer starting at 54 and moving in left direction. Find the number of head movements in cylinders using C LOOK scheduling.

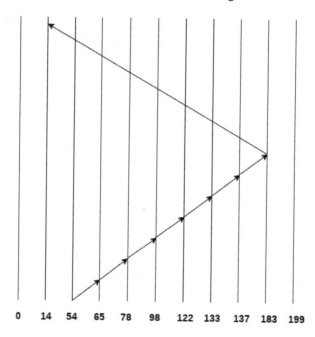

Number of cylinders crossed = 11 + 13 + 20 + 24 + 11 + 4 + 46 + 169 = 298

Numerical on SSTF and SCAN

Question
Suppose the following disk request sequence (track numbers) for a disk with 100 tracks is given: 45, 20, 90, 10, 50, 60, 80 and 70. Assume that the initial position of the R/W head is on track 50. The additional distance that will be traversed by the R/W head when the Shortest Seek Time First (SSTF) algorithm is used compared to the SCAN (Elevator) algorithm (assuming that SCAN algorithm moves towards 100 when it starts execution) is _____ tracks

(A) 5
(B) 9
(C) 10
(D) 11

Using SSTF Algorithm
Number of track are 100.
Initial Position of R/W head is 50.
The requests are: 45, 20, 90, 10, 50, 60, 80 and 70

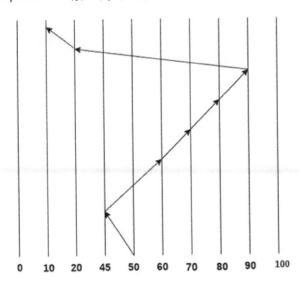

Number of crossed cylinders = 5 + 15 + 10 + 10 + 10 + 70 + 10 = 130

Using SCAN Algorithm

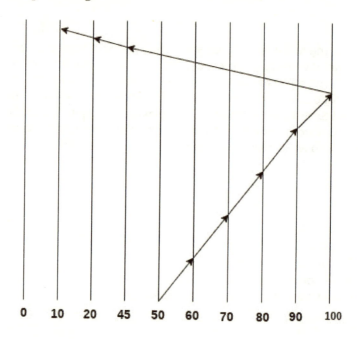

Number of cylinders crosses
= 0 + 10 + 10 + 10 + 10 + 10 + 55 + 20 + 10
= 135

Therefore the answer is (A). The SCAN algorithm travels for 5 additional tracks.

Numerical on Disk Scheduling Algorithms

Consider a disk with 200 tracks and the queue has random requests from different processes in the order:
+55, 58, 39, 18, 90, 160, 150, 38, 184

Initially arm is at 100. Find the Average Seek length using FIFO, SSTF, SCAN and C-SCAN algorithm.

Solution

Using FCFS		Using SSTF		Using SCAN		Using C - SCAN	
Next request to be serviced	No. of cylinders travelled	Next request to be serviced	No. of cylinders travelled	Next request to be serviced	No. of cylinders travelled	Next request to be serviced	No. of cylinders travelled
55	45	90	10	150	50	150	50
58	3	58	32	160	10	160	10
39	19	55	3	184	24	184	24
18	21	39	16	90	94	18	166
90	72	38	1	58	32	38	20
160	70	18	20	55	3	39	1
150	10	150	132	39	16	55	16
38	112	160	10	38	1	58	3
184	146	184	24	18	20	90	32
Average Seek Length	498 / 9 = 55.3	Average Seek Length	27.5	Average Seek Length	27.8	Average Seek Length	35.6

Chapter 8 - Unix Based C-

Programs

Program - ex1a.c

```c
#include<stdio.h>
#include<stdlib.h>
#include<unistd.h>
#include<string.h>
#include<sys/wait.h>

int main(int argc, char*argv[])
{
        int pid;
        char s[100];
        pid=fork();
        argv[2]="date";
        if(pid<0)
        printf("Error.");

        else if(pid>0)
        {
                wait(NULL);
                printf("\nParent process\n");
                printf("\nParent process ID : %d\n\n",getpid());
                execlp("stat","stat","ex1a.c",NULL);
                exit(0);
        }
        else
        {
                printf("\nChild process\n");
                printf("\nChild process parent ID : %d\n",getppid());
                printf("\nChild process ID : %d\n\n",getpid());
                execvp(argv[2],argv);
                close(pid);

        }
```

```
                return 0;
}
```

Output

```
oem@RobertKaramagi ~ $ cd lab
oem@RobertKaramagi ~/lab $ gcc ex1a.c -o ex1a
oem@RobertKaramagi ~/lab $ ./ex1a

Child process

Child process parent ID : 13981

Child process ID : 13982

Tue Nov 29 18:16:37 EAT 2016

Parent process

Parent process ID : 13981

  File: 'ex1a.c'
  Size: 615            Blocks: 8        IO Block: 4096    regular file
Device: 808h/2056d     Inode: 544511    Links: 2
Access: (0644/-rw-r--r--)  Uid: (29999/    oem)   Gid: (29999/     oem)
Access: 2016-11-29 18:16:35.985235407 +0300
Modify: 2016-11-29 18:16:26.209235157 +0300
Change: 2016-11-29 18:16:26.209235157 +0300
 Birth: -
oem@RobertKaramagi ~/lab $ ▯
```

UNIX System Calls: opendir, readdir (ls)

Program - ex1b.c

```c
#include<stdio.h>
#include<stdlib.h>
#include<sys/types.h>
#include<dirent.h>

int main(int argc,char* argv[])
{
        DIR *d;
        struct dirent *r;
        int i=0;
        d=opendir(".");
        if(d==NULL)
        {
                printf("Error! Unable to open directory.\n");
                exit(1);
        }
        printf("\n\t Name of file \n");
        while((r=readdir(d)) != NULL)
        {
```

```
                    printf("\t$ %s \n",r->d_name);
                    i=i+1;
            }
            closedir(d);
            printf("\n The total number of files in the directory is %d \n\n",i);
            return 0;
}
```

Output

```
oem@RobertKaramagi ~/lab
File  Edit  View  Search  Terminal  Help
oem@RobertKaramagi ~ $ cd lab
oem@RobertKaramagi ~/lab $ gcc ex1b.c -o ex1b
oem@RobertKaramagi ~/lab $ ls -a
.    ex1a     ex1b     ex2     file     LC_PAPER=sw_TZ
     ex1a.c   ex1b.c   ex2.c   file.c   robert.txt
oem@RobertKaramagi ~/lab $ ./ex1b

        Name of file
        $ file
        $ ex1a.c
        $ ex1b
        $ ex1a
        $ LC_PAPER=sw_TZ
        $ ex2
        $ .
        $ robert.txt
        $ ..
        $ ex2.c
        $ ex1b.c
        $ file.c

 The total number of files in the directory is 12

oem@RobertKaramagi ~/lab $ []
```

UNIX System Calls: open, read, write

Program – ex2.c

```
#include<stdio.h>
#include<stdlib.h>
#include<sys/types.h>
#include<sys/stat.h>
#include<fcntl.h>
#include<unistd.h>
#include<time.h>

int main(int argc,char*argv[])
{
        char buf[100];
        struct stat s;
        int fd,n;
```

```
fd=open(argv[1], O_WRONLY,0777);
fd=creat(argv[2],O_RDONLY);
stat(argv[2],&s);
if(fd==-1)
printf("Error in Creation.");
while( ( n=read(fd,buf,sizeof(buf)) ) > 0 )
{
            if(write(fd,buf,n)!=n)
            {
                        close(fd);
            }
}
printf("\n\t$User ID for file: %d \n",s.st_uid);
printf("\n\t$File access time: %s \n",ctime(&s.st_atime));
printf("\n\t$File modification time: %s \n",ctime(&s.st_mtime));
printf("\n\t$File index node number: %ld \n",s.st_ino);
printf("\n\t$Permission for file: %o \n\n",s.st_mode);
return 0;
}
}
```

Output

Unix commands: ls, grep

Program – ex3.c

```
#include <sys/types.h>
#include <sys/dir.h>
#include <sys/param.h>
#include <stdio.h>
```

```c
#include <stdlib.h>
#include<string.h>

void grep();

int main(int argc, char* argv[])
{
        int n;
        while(1)
        {
                printf("\nEnter an option.\n");
                printf("\n1.Unix command ls.");
                printf("\n2.Unix command grep.");
                printf("\n3.Unix command cp.");
                printf("\n4.Unix command rm.\n");
                scanf("%d",&n);
                switch(n)
                {
                        case 1:
                                system("ls");
                                break;

                        case 2:
                                grep();
                                break;

                        case 3:
                                system("cp -l ex3.c copy.c");
                                printf("The file has been copied
                                succesfully.");
                                break;

                        case 4:
                                system("rm copy.c");
                                printf("The file has been removed
                                succesfully.");
                                break;

                        default:
                                printf("Invalid choice.\n");
                                exit(0);
                                break;
                }
        }
        return 0;
}
```

```
void grep()
{
        char fn[10],pat[10],temp[200];
        FILE *fp;
        printf("Enter file name\n");
        scanf("%s",fn);
        printf("Enter pattern to be searched\n");
        scanf("%s",pat);
        fp=fopen(fn,"r");
        while(!feof(fp))
        {
                fgets(temp,1000,fp);
                if(strstr(temp,pat))
                printf("%s",temp);
        }
        fclose(fp);
}
```

Output

```
oem@RobertKaramagi ~ $ cd lab
oem@RobertKaramagi ~/lab $ gcc ex3.c -o ex3
oem@RobertKaramagi ~/lab $ ./ex3

Enter an option.

1.Unix command ls.
2.Unix command grep.
3.Unix command cp.
4.Unix command rm.
1
date     ex1b     ex2.c   ex4a     ex4b.c  ex5b      ex6.c
ex1a     ex1b.c   ex3     ex4a.c   ex5a    ex5b.c  LC_PAPER=sw_TZ
ex1a.c   ex2      ex3.c   ex4b     ex5a.c  ex6

Enter an option.

1.Unix command ls.
2.Unix command grep.
3.Unix command cp.
4.Unix command rm.
2
Enter file name
ex3.c
Enter pattern to be searched
fp
        FILE *fp;
        fp=fopen(fn,"r");
        while(!feof(fp))
                fgets(temp,1000,fp);
        fclose(fp);

Enter an option.

1.Unix command ls.
2.Unix command grep.
3.Unix command cp.
4.Unix command rm.
3
The file has been copied succesfully.
Enter an option.
```

```
1.Unix command ls.
2.Unix command grep.
3.Unix command cp.
4.Unix command rm.
1
copy.c  exla.c  ex2    ex3.c  ex4b    ex5a.c  ex6
date    ex1b    ex2.c  ex4a   ex4b.c  ex5b    ex6.c
exla    ex1b.c  ex3    ex4a.c ex5a    ex5b.c  LC_PAPER=sw_TZ

Enter an option.

1.Unix command ls.
2.Unix command grep.
3.Unix command cp.
4.Unix command rm.
4
The file has been removed succesfully.
Enter an option.

1.Unix command ls.
2.Unix command grep.
3.Unix command cp.
4.Unix command rm.
1
date    ex1b    ex2.c  ex4a   ex4b.c  ex5b    ex6.c
exla    ex1b.c  ex3    ex4a.c ex5a    ex5b.c  LC_PAPER=sw_TZ
exla.c  ex2     ex3.c  ex4b   ex5a.c  ex6

Enter an option.

1.Unix command ls.
2.Unix command grep.
3.Unix command cp.
4.Unix command rm.
5
Invalid choice.
oem@RobertKaramagi ~/lab $ |
```

First Come First Served Scheduling

Program – ex4a.c

```c
#include<stdio.h>
#include<stdlib.h>

int main() {
        int n, a[10], b[10], t[10], w[10], g[10], i,j,k;
        float att=0, awt=0;
        for(i=0;i<10;i++)
```

```c
        a[i]=b[i]=t[i]=w[i]=g[i]=0;
printf("\nEnter the number of processes.\n");
scanf("%d",&n);
printf("\nEnter the burst times.\n");
for(i=0;i<n;i++)
        scanf("%d",&b[i]);
printf("\nEnter the arrival times.\n");
for(i=0;i<n;i++)
        scanf("%d",&a[i]);
for(i=0;i<n;i++)
        g[i+1]=g[i]+b[i];
for(i=0;i<n;i++)
{
        w[i]=g[i]-a[i];
        t[i]=g[i+1]-a[i];
        awt=awt+w[i];
        att=att+t[i];
}
awt=awt/n;
att=att/n;
puts("\n\n+---------+-----------+--------------+----------------+-----------------+");
puts("| Process | Burst Time | Arrival Time | Waiting Time | Turn around
Time |");
puts("+---------+-----------+--------------+----------------+-----------------+");
for(i=0; i<n; i++)
{
        printf("| P%2d |  %2d   |   %2d    |   %2d   |   %2d    |\n"
                ,i+1,b[i],a[i],w[i],t[i]);
        puts("+---------+-----------+--------------+----------------+-----------------+");
}
puts("\n\nGANTT CHART");
puts("***********");

// print top bar
printf(" ");
for(i=0; i<n; i++)
{
        for(j=0; j<b[i]; j++)
                printf("--");
        printf(" ");
}
printf("\n|");

// printing process id in the middle
for(i=0; i<n; i++)
{
        for(j=0; j<b[i]-1; j++)  printf(" ");
```

```c
                          printf("P%d", i+1);
              for(j=0; j<b[i]-1; j++)
                              printf(" ");
              printf("|");
    }
  printf("\n ");

  // printing bottom bar
  for(i=0; i<n; i++)
  {
              for(j=0; j<b[i]; j++)
                              printf("--");
              printf(" ");
  }
  printf("\n");

  // printing the time line
  printf("o");
  for(i=0; i<n; i++)
  {
              for(j=0; j<b[i]; j++)
                              printf(" ");
              if(g[i] > 9)
                              printf("\b"); // backspace : remove 1 space
              printf("%d", g[i+1]);
  }
  printf("\n");
  printf("\n\nAverage waiting time: %f ms\n",awt);
  printf("\nAverage turn around time: %f ms\n",att);
  return 0;
}
```

Output

```
+----------+------------+--------------+--------------+------------------+
| Process  | Burst Time | Arrival Time | Waiting Time | Turn around Time |
+----------+------------+--------------+--------------+------------------+
|  P 1     |     4      |      0       |      0       |        4         |
+----------+------------+--------------+--------------+------------------+
|  P 2     |     9      |      2       |      2       |       11         |
+----------+------------+--------------+--------------+------------------+
|  P 3     |     8      |      4       |      9       |       17         |
+----------+------------+--------------+--------------+------------------+
|  P 4     |    13      |      3       |     18       |       31         |
+----------+------------+--------------+--------------+------------------+

GANTT CHART
***********

    --------   -----------------   -----------------   -----------------
|    P1    |        P2         |        P3         |        P4         |
    --------   -----------------   -----------------   -----------------
0         4                   13                  21                  34

Average waiting time: 7.250000 ms

Average turn around time: 15.750000 ms
oem@RobertKaramagi ~/lab $ []
```

Shortest Job First Scheduling

Program – ex4b.c

```c
#include<stdio.h>
#include<stdlib.h>

int main()
{
        int i,j,n,temp,temp1,b[10],t[10],w[10],p[10];
        float att=0,awt=0;
        for(i=0;i<10;i++)
                b[i]=t[i]=w[i]=p[i]=0;
        printf("\nEnter the number of processes.\n");
        scanf("%d",&n);
        printf("\nEnter the burst times.\n");

        for(i=0;i<n;i++)
        {
                printf("P[%d] : ", i+1);
                scanf("%d", &b[i]);
        }

        for(i=0;i<n-1;i++)
        {
                for(j=i+1;j<n;j++)
                {
                        if(b[i]>b[j])
```

```c
                    {
                            temp=b[i];

                            temp1=p[i];

                            b[i]=b[j];
                            p[i]=p[j];
                            b[j]=temp;

                            p[j]=temp1;
                    }
            }
    }

    w[0]=0;

    for(i=0;i<n;i++)
    {
            w[i+1]=w[i]+b[i];
            t[i]=w[i]+b[i];
            awt=awt+w[i];
            att=att+t[i];
    }

    puts("\n\n+--------+----------+------------+-----------------+");
    puts("| Process | Burst Time | Waiting Time | Turn around Time |");
    puts("+--------+----------+------------+-----------------+");

    for(i=0; i<n; i++)
    {
            printf("|  P%2d  |   %2d   |   %2d   |     %2d    |\n"
                        ,i+1,b[i],w[i],t[i]);
            puts("+--------+----------+------------+-----------------+");
    }

    puts("\n\nGANTT CHART");
    puts("***********");
    // print top bar
    printf(" ");

    for(i=0; i<n; i++)
    {
            for(j=0; j<b[i]; j++)
                    printf("--");
            printf(" ");
    }
    printf("\n|");
```

```c
        // printing process id in the middle
        for(i=0; i<n; i++)
        {
                for(j=0; j<b[i]-1; j++)
                        printf(" ");
                printf("P%d", i+1);
                for(j=0; j<b[i]-1; j++)
                        printf(" ");
                printf("|");
        }
        printf("\n ");

// printing bottom bar
        for(i=0; i<n; i++)
        {
                for(j=0; j<b[i]; j++)
                        printf("--");
                printf(" ");
        }
        printf("\n");

        // printing the time line
        printf("0");

        for(i=0; i<n; i++)
        {
                for(j=0; j<b[i]; j++)
                        printf("  ");
                if(t[i] > 9)
                        printf("\b"); // backspace : remove 1 space
                printf("%d", t[i]);
        }

         printf("\n");

        printf("\n\nAverage waiting time: %f ms\n",awt);
        printf("\nAverage turn around time: %f ms\n",att);
        return 0;
}
```

Output

```
oem@RobertKaramagi ~ $ cd lab
oem@RobertKaramagi ~/lab $ gcc ex4b.c -o ex4b
oem@RobertKaramagi ~/lab $ ./ex4b

Enter the number of processes.
5

Enter the burst times.
P[1] : 3
P[2] : 2
P[3] : 6
P[4] : 4
P[5] : 5
```

```
+---------+-----------+--------------+------------------+
| Process | Burst Time | Waiting Time | Turn around Time |
+---------+-----------+--------------+------------------+
|   P 1   |     2     |      0       |        2         |
+---------+-----------+--------------+------------------+
|   P 2   |     3     |      2       |        5         |
+---------+-----------+--------------+------------------+
|   P 3   |     4     |      5       |        9         |
+---------+-----------+--------------+------------------+
|   P 4   |     5     |      9       |       14         |
+---------+-----------+--------------+------------------+
|   P 5   |     6     |     14       |       20         |
+---------+-----------+--------------+------------------+
```

```
GANTT CHART
***********

 ----  ------  --------  -----------  -----------
| P1 |  P2   |   P3    |     P4      |    P5      |
 ----  ------  --------  -----------  -----------
0      2       5         9           14          20
```

```
Average waiting time: 30.000000 ms

Average turn around time: 50.000000 ms
oem@RobertKaramagi ~/lab $ ▯
```

Round Robin Scheduling

Program – ex5a.c

```c
#include<stdio.h>
#include<stdlib.h>
```

```c
int main() {
        int
i,j,k,n,bt[20],gc[20],wt[20],tat[20],bt1[20],st[20],ts,count=0,sum_bt=0,tq;
        int swt=0,stat=0,temp,sq=0,c,p=0;
        float awt=0.0,atat=0.0;
        printf("\nEnter the number of processs: ");
        scanf("%d",&n);
        printf("\nEnter the burst times:\n");
        for(i=0; i<n; i++)
        {
                scanf("%d",&bt[i]);
                bt1[i]=bt[i];
                st[i]=bt[i];
        }

        printf("\nEnter the time slice.\n");
        scanf("%d",&ts);
        tq=ts;
        for(i=0; i<n; i++)
                sum_bt=sum_bt+bt[i];
        for(k=0; k<n; k++)
        {
                do
                {
                        for(i=0; i<n; i++)
                        {
                                if(bt[i]>=ts)
                                {
                                for(j=count; j<(count+ts); j++)
                                                gc[j]=i+1;

                                        count+=ts;
                                bt[i]=bt[i]-ts;
                                }
                                else
                                {
                                        for(j=count; j<=(count+bt[i]);
                                        j++)
                                        gc[j]=i+1;

                                        count+=bt[i];

                                        bt[i]=0;
                                }
                        }
                }while(bt[k]!=0);
```

```c
        }

        while(1)
        {
                for(i=0,count=0;i<n;i++)
                {
                        temp=tq;
                        if(st[i]==0)
                        {
                                count++;
                                continue;
                        }
                        if(st[i]>tq)
                                st[i]=st[i]-tq;

                                else if(st[i]>=0)
                                {
                                        temp=st[i];
                                        st[i]=0;
                                }
                                sq=sq+temp;
                                tat[i]=sq;
                }
                if(n==count)
                        break;
        }

        for(i=0;i<n;i++)
        {
                wt[i]=tat[i]-bt1[i];
                swt=swt+wt[i];
                stat=stat+tat[i];
        }
        awt=(float)swt/n;
        atat=(float)stat/n;
        puts("\n\n+--------+----------+------------+-----------------+");
        puts("| Process | Burst Time | Waiting Time | Turn around Time |");
        puts("+--------+----------+------------+-----------------+");

        for(i=0;i<n;i++)
        {
                printf("|  %2d  |   %2d   |   %2d   |    %2d    |\n"
                        ,i+1,bt1[i],wt[i],tat[i]);
                puts("+--------+----------+------------+-----------------+");
        }

        printf("\nAverage waiting time: %f ms\n",awt);
```

```c
        printf("\nAverage Turn around time: %f ms\n",atat);
        puts("\n\nGANTT CHART");
        puts("***********");
        c=gc[o];
        printf("==========================================\n");
        printf("| P%d |",gc[o]);
        for(i=1;i<sum_bt;i++)
        {
                if(gc[i]!=c)
                {
                        printf(" P%d |",gc[i]);
                        c=gc[i];
                }
        }
         printf("\n========================================");
        printf("\no    ");
        c=gc[o];
        for(i=1;i<=sum_bt;i++)
        {
                p=p+1;
                if(gc[i]!=c)
                {
                        printf("%d    ",p);
                        c=gc[i];
                }
        }
        printf("\n");
return 0;
}
```

Output

```
+----------+------------+--------------+------------------+
| Process  | Burst Time | Waiting Time | Turn around Time |
+----------+------------+--------------+------------------+
|    1     |     2      |      0       |        2         |
+----------+------------+--------------+------------------+
|    2     |     3      |      6       |        9         |
+----------+------------+--------------+------------------+
|    3     |     3      |      7       |        10        |
+----------+------------+--------------+------------------+
|    4     |     2      |      6       |        8         |
+----------+------------+--------------+------------------+
```

Average waiting time: 4.750000 ms

Average Turn around time: 7.250000 ms

GANTT CHART
****

```
=================================================
|  P1  |  P2  |  P3  |  P4  |  P2  |  P3  |
=================================================
0      2      4      6      8     9      10
```
oem@RobertKaramagi ~/lab $ []

Priority Scheduling

Program – ex5b.c

```c
#include<stdio.h>
#include<stdio.h>

int main()
{
        int i,j,n,temp,temp1,temp2,pr[10],b[10],t[10],w[10],p[10];
        float att=0,awt=0;
        printf("\nEnter the number of processes.");
        scanf("%d",&n);
        printf("\nEnter the burst times.\n");

        for(i=0;i<n;i++)
        {
                scanf("%d",&b[i]);
                p[i]=i;
        }
        printf("\nEnter the priority.\n");
        for(i=0;i<n;i++)
        {
                scanf("%d",&pr[i]);
```

```c
}
for(i=0;i<n-1;i++)
{
        for(j=i+1;j<n;j++)
        {
                if(pr[i]>pr[j])
                {
                        temp=b[i];

                        temp1=p[i];

                        temp2=pr[i];

                        b[i]=b[j];
                        p[i]=p[j];
                        pr[i]=pr[j];

                        b[j]=temp;

                        p[j]=temp1;
                        pr[j]=temp2;
                }
        }
}
w[0]=0;

for(i=0;i<n;i++)
        w[i+1]=w[i]+b[i];
for(i=0;i<n;i++)
{
        t[i]=w[i]+b[i];
        awt=awt+w[i];
        att=att+t[i];
}

awt=awt/n;
att=att/n;
puts("\n\n+--------+-----------+-------------+------------------+");
puts("| Process | Burst Time | Waiting Time | Turn around Time |");
puts("+--------+-----------+-------------+------------------+");

for(i=0; i<n; i++)
{
        printf("|  %2d  |   %2d   |   %2d   |    %2d    |\n"
                ,i+1,b[i],w[i],t[i]);
        puts("+--------+-----------+-------------+------------------+");
}
```

```c
puts("\n\nGANTT CHART");
puts("***********");

// print top bar
printf(" ");

for(i=0; i<n; i++)
{
        for(j=0; j<b[i]; j++)
                  printf("--");
        printf(" ");
}
printf("\n|");

// printing process id in the middle
for(i=0; i<n; i++)
{
        for(j=0; j<b[i]-1; j++)
                  printf("  ");
        printf("P%d", i+1);
        for(j=0; j<b[i]-1; j++)
                  printf("  ");
        printf("|");
}
printf("\n ");

// printing bottom bar
for(i=0; i<n; i++)
{
        for(j=0; j<b[i]; j++)
                  printf("--");
        printf(" ");
}
printf("\n");

// printing the time line
printf("0");

for(i=0; i<n; i++)
{
        for(j=0; j<b[i]; j++)
                  printf("  ");
        if(t[i] > 9)
                  printf("\b"); // backspace : remove 1 space
        printf("%d", t[i]);

}
```

```
            printf("\n");

        printf("\n\nAverage waiting time: %f ms\n",awt);
        printf("\nAverage turn around time: %f ms\n",att);      return o;
}
```

Output

Program – ex6.c

```c
#include<stdio.h>
#include<stdlib.h>
#include<unistd.h>
#include<fcntl.h>

int main(int argc, char* argv[])
{
        int pid,pfd[2],n,a,b,c;

        if(pipe(pfd)==-1)
        {
                printf("\nError in pipe connection\n");
                exit(1);
        }

        pid=fork();

        if(pid>0)
        {
                puts("\nParent Process");
                puts("\n**************");
                printf("\n\n\tFibonacci Series");
                printf("\nEnter the limit for the series:");
                scanf("%d",&n);
                write(pfd[1],&n,sizeof(n));
                close(pfd[1]);
                exit(0);
        }

        else
        {
                read(pfd[0],&n,sizeof(n));
                puts("\nChild Process");
                puts("\n**************");
                a=0;
                b=1;
                close(pfd[0]);
                printf("\nFibonacci Series is:");
                printf("\n\n%d\n%d",a,b);

                while(n>2)
                {
                        c=a+b;
```

```
                    printf("\n%d",c);
                    a=b;
                    b=c;
                    n--;
          }

    }

    puts("\n");
    return 0;

}
```

Output

```
File  Edit  View  Search  Terminal  Help
oem@RobertKaramagi ~ $ cd lab
oem@RobertKaramagi ~/lab $ gcc ex6.c -o ex6
oem@RobertKaramagi ~/lab $ ./ex6

Parent Process

**************


        Fibonacci Series
Enter the limit for the series:25

Child Process

**************

Fibonacci Series is:

0
1
1
2
3
5
8
13
21
34
55
89
144
233
377
610
987
1597
2584
4181
6765
10946
17711
28657
46368
```

Program – ex7.c

```c
#include<stdio.h>
#include<stdlib.h>
#include<semaphore.h>
#include<pthread.h>

int mutex=1,full=0,empty=3,x=0;

int main()
{
        int n;
        void producer();
        void consumer();
        int wait(int);
        int signal(int);
        printf("\n 1.Producer \n 2.Consumer \n 3.Exit");

        while(1)
        {
                printf("\n\n Enter your choice:");
                scanf("%d",&n);

                switch(n)
                {
                        case 1:
                                if((mutex==1)&&(empty!=0))

                                        producer();
                                else
                                        printf(" Buffer is full");
                                break;

                        case 2:
                                if((mutex==1)&&(full!=0))
                                        consumer();

                                else
                                        printf(" Buffer is empty");
                                break;

                        case 3:
                                exit(0);
                                break;
                }
```

```
                }
}

int wait(int s)
{
            return (--s);
}


int signal(int s)
{
            return(++s);
}


void producer()
{
            mutex=wait(mutex);
            full=signal(full);
            empty=wait(empty);
            x++;
            printf(" Producer produces the item %d",x);
            mutex=signal(mutex);
}

void consumer()
{
            mutex=wait(mutex);
            full=wait(full);
            empty=signal(empty);
            printf(" Consumer consumes item %d",x);
            x--;
            mutex=signal(mutex);
}
```

Output

File Edit View Search Terminal Help
```
oem@RobertKaramagi ~ $ cd lab
oem@RobertKaramagi ~/lab $ gcc ex7.c -o ex7
oem@RobertKaramagi ~/lab $ ./ex7

1.Producer
2.Consumer
3.Exit

Enter your choice:1
Producer produces the item 1

Enter your choice:1
Producer produces the item 2
```

```
Enter your choice:1
Producer produces the item 3

Enter your choice:1
Buffer is full

Enter your choice:2
Consumer consumes item 3

Enter your choice:2
Consumer consumes item 2

Enter your choice:2
Consumer consumes item 1

Enter your choice:2
Buffer is empty

Enter your choice:3
oem@RobertKaramagi ~/lab $ █
```

First Fit Memory Management Scheme

Program – ex8.c

```c
#include<stdio.h>
#include<stdlib.h>

struct firstfit
{
        int b[20],p[20];
} *ptr,*ptr1;

int i,j,n,m;

void display(struct firstfit *disp);

int main() {

        printf("\nEnter the number of Blocks: ");
        scanf("%d",&n);

        ptr=(struct firstfit*)malloc(n*sizeof(struct firstfit));
        printf("\nEnter the size of the Blocks.\n");

        for(i=0;i<n;i++)
        {
                printf("Block [%d]: ",i);
                scanf("%d", &(ptr+i)->b[i]);
        }

        printf("\nEnter the number of Processes: ");
```

```c
            scanf("%d",&m);
            ptr1=(struct firstfit*)malloc(m*sizeof(struct firstfit));
            printf("\nEnter the size of the Processes.\n");

            for(i=0;i<m;i++)
            {
                    printf("Process [%d]: ",i);
                    scanf("%d", &(ptr1+i)->p[i]);
            }

            struct firstfit disp;

            display(&disp);

}

void display(struct firstfit *disp)
{
            for(i=0;i<n;i++)
            {
                    for(j=0;j<m;j++)
                    {
                            if((ptr1+j)->p[j] <= (ptr+i)->b[i])
                            {
                                    printf("\nThe Process %d is allocated to
                                    Block %d\n",j, i);
                                    (ptr1+j)->p[j]=10000;

                                    break;
                            }
                    }
            }

            for(j=0;j<m;j++)
            {
                    if((ptr1+j)->p[j] != 10000)
                    {
                            printf("\nThe Process %d is not allocated\n",j);
                    }
            }
}
```

Output

```
oem@RobertKaramagi ~ $ cd lab
oem@RobertKaramagi ~/lab $ gcc ex8.c -o ex8
oem@RobertKaramagi ~/lab $ ./ex8

Enter the number of Blocks: 5

Enter the size of the Blocks.
Block [0]: 10
Block [1]: 20
Block [2]: 10
Block [3]: 15
Block [4]: 25

Enter the number of Processes: 5

Enter the size of the Processes.
Process [0]: 20
Process [1]: 10
Process [2]: 15
Process [3]: 10
Process [4]: 35

The Process 1 is allocated to Block 0

The Process 0 is allocated to Block 1

The Process 3 is allocated to Block 2

The Process 2 is allocated to Block 3

The Process 4 is not allocated
oem@RobertKaramagi ~/lab $ ▮
```

Best Fit Memory Management Scheme

Program – ex8.c

```c
#include<stdio.h>
#include<stdlib.h>

struct bestfit
{
        int b[20],p[20],b1[20],p1[20];
}*ptr,*ptr1;

int i,j,n,m;
void display(struct bestfit *disp);

int main()
{
```

```c
        int temp,temp1,temp2;
        printf("\nEnter the number of Blocks: ");
        scanf("%d",&n);
        ptr=(struct bestfit*)malloc(n*sizeof(struct bestfit));
        printf("\nEnter the size of the Blocks.\n");

        for(i=0;i<n;i++)
        {
                printf("Block [%d]: ",i);
                scanf("%d", &(ptr+i)->b[i]);
                (ptr+i)->b1[i]=i;
        }

        printf("\nEnter the number of Processes: ");
        scanf("%d",&m);
        ptr1=(struct bestfit*)malloc(m*sizeof(struct bestfit));
        printf("\nEnter the size of the Processes.\n");

        for(i=0;i<m;i++)
        {
                printf("Process [%d]: ",i);
                scanf("%d", &(ptr1+i)->p[i]);
                (ptr1+i)->p1[i]=i;
        }

        struct bestfit dlsp;
        display(&disp);
}

void display(struct bestfit *disp)
{

        for(i=0;i<n;i++)
        {
                for(j=0;j<m;j++)
                {
                        if((ptr1+j)->p[j] <= (ptr+i)->b[i])
                        {
                                printf("\nThe Process %d is allocated to Block
                                %d\n",(ptr1+j)->p1[j],(ptr+i)->b1[i]);
                                        (ptr1+j)->p[j]=10000;

                                break;
                        }
                }
        }
        for(j=0;j<m;j++)
```

```
                {
                        if((ptr1+j)->p[j] != 10000)
                        {
                                printf("\nThe Process %d is not allocated\n",j);
                        }
                }
        }
}
```

Output

```
File  Edit  View  Search  Terminal  Help
oem@RobertKaramagi ~ $ cd lab
oem@RobertKaramagi ~/lab $ gcc ex9a.c -o ex9a
oem@RobertKaramagi ~/lab $ ./ex9a

Enter the number of Blocks: 5

Enter the size of the Blocks.
Block [0]: 10
Block [1]: 20
Block [2]: 30
Block [3]: 40
Block [4]: 50

Enter the number of Processes: 5

Enter the size of the Processes.
Process [0]: 47
Process [1]: 28
Process [2]: 36
Process [3]: 4
Process [4]: 15

The Process 3 is allocated to Block 0

The Process 4 is allocated to Block 1

The Process 1 is allocated to Block 2

The Process 2 is allocated to Block 3

The Process 0 is allocated to Block 4
oem@RobertKaramagi ~/lab $ █
```

Worst Fit Memory Management Scheme

Program – ex9b.c

```
#include<stdio.h>
#include<stdlib.h>

struct worstfit
{
        int p[20],p1[20],p2[20],b[20],frag[20],bf[20],ff[20];
} *ptr, wf;
```

```c
int i,m;
void display(struct worstfit *disp);

int main()
{
        int j,n,temp,highest=0;
        printf("\nEnter the number of Blocks: ");
        scanf("%d",&n);
        printf("\nEnter the size of the Blocks.\n");

        for(i=1;i<=n;i++)
        {
                printf("Block [%d]: ",i);
                scanf("%d", &wf.b[i]);
        }

        printf("\nEnter the number of Processes: ");
        scanf("%d",&m);
        ptr=(struct worstfit*)malloc(m*sizeof(struct worstfit));
        printf("\nEnter the size of the Processes.\n");

        for(i=1;i<=m;i++)
        {
                printf("Process [%d]: ",i);
                scanf("%d", &wf.p[i]);
                (ptr+i)->p1[i]=wf.p[i];
                (ptr+i)->p2[i]=i;
        }

        for(i=1;i<=n;i++)
        {
                for(j=1;j<=m;j++)
                {
                        if(wf.bf[j]!=1)
                        {
                                temp= wf.b[j]-wf.p[i];

                                if(temp>=0)
                                        if(highest<temp)
                                        {
                                                wf.ff[i]=j;
                                                highest=temp;
                                        }
                        }
                }
                wf.frag[i]=highest;
                wf.bf[wf.ff[i]]=1;
```

```c
                        highest=0;
                }

                struct worstfit disp;
                display(&disp);
                return 0;
        }

void display(struct worstfit *disp)
{
                puts("\n\n+------+-----------+----+----------+-------+");
                puts("|Process|Process size|Block|Block Size|Fragment|");
                puts("+------+-----------+----+----------+-------+");

                for(i=1;i<=m;i++)
                {
                        printf("| %2d  |   %2d   |%2d  |  %2d   | %2d  |"
                                        ,(ptr+i)->p2[i],(ptr+i)->p1[i],wf.ff[i],
                                        wf.b[wf.ff[i]]
                                        ,wf.frag[i]);
                        puts("\n+------+-----------+----+----------+-------+");
                }

                printf("\n");
}
```

Output

```
File  Edit  View  Search  Terminal  Help
oem@RobertKaramagi ~ $ cd lab
oem@RobertKaramagi ~/lab $ gcc ex9b.c -o ex9b
oem@RobertKaramagi ~/lab $ ./ex9b

Enter the number of Blocks: 3

Enter the size of the Blocks.
Block [1]: 20
Block [2]: 30
Block [3]: 10

Enter the number of Processes: 3

Enter the size of the Processes.
Process [1]: 10
Process [2]: 14
Process [3]: 6


+-------+------------+-----+-----------+--------+
|Process|Process size|Block|Block Size|Fragment|
+-------+------------+-----+-----------+--------+
|   1   |     10     |  2  |    30     |   20   |
+-------+------------+-----+-----------+--------+
|   2   |     14     |  1  |    20     |   6    |
+-------+------------+-----+-----------+--------+
|   3   |     6      |  3  |    10     |   4    |
+-------+------------+-----+-----------+--------+

oem@RobertKaramagi ~/lab $
```

Program - ex10.c

```c
#include<stdio.h>
#include<stdlib.h>

int main()
{
        int n, fc[20], mb[100], i, j, k, fb[100], fs[20], mc=0;
        printf("\nEnter the number of files: ");
        scanf("%d",&n);

        for(i=0;i<n;i++)
        {
                printf("\nEnter the capacity of file %d: ",i+1);
                scanf("%d",&fc[i]);
                printf("\nEnter the starting address of file %d: ",i+1);
                scanf("%d",&fs[i]);
        }

        printf("\n\nCONTIGUOUS FILE ALLOCATION");
        printf("\n*************************\n");

        for(i=0;i<100;i++)
                fb[i]=1;

        for(i=0;i<n;i++)
        {
                j=fs[i];
                {
                        if(fb[j]==1)
                        {
                                for(k=j;k<(j+fc[i]);k++)
                                {
                                        if(fb[k]==1)
                                        mc++;
                                }

                                if(mc==fc[i])
                                {
                                        for(k=fs[i];k<(fs[i]+fc[i]);k++)
                                        {
                                                fb[k]=0;
                                        }
```

```
                                                    printf("\nFile %d is allocated
                                                    from address %d t %d.\n"
                                                            ,i+1,fs[i],fs[i]+fc[i]-1);
                                        }
                        }
                        else
                                        printf("\nFile %d is not allocated since
contiguous memory of size %d is not

available from address
%d.\n",i+1,fc[i],fs[i]);
                        }
                        mc=0;
                }
                printf("\n\n");           return 0;
}
```

Output

Chapter 9 - Shell Script

Programs

#Factorial of a given number

ex11.sh

#!bin/bash

```
echo "Enter the number"
read n
i=1
fact=1
while [ $i -le $n ]
do
((fact=$fact*$i))
((i=$i+1))
done
echo "Factorial of $n is: $fact"
```

Output

```
                    robertkaramagi@robertkaramagi ~/lab        _ + x
File Edit View Search Terminal Help
robertkaramagi@robertkaramagi ~ $ cd lab
robertkaramagi@robertkaramagi ~/lab $ chmod +x ex11.sh
robertkaramagi@robertkaramagi ~/lab $ ls -l ex11.sh
-rwxr-xr-x 1 robertkaramagi robertkaramagi 175 Jan  6 20:27 ex11.sh
robertkaramagi@robertkaramagi ~/lab $ bash ex11.sh
Enter the number
6
Factorial of 6 is: 720
robertkaramagi@robertkaramagi ~/lab $ []
```

ex12.sh

```
#!bin/bash

echo "Enter the value of m"
read m
echo "Enter the value of n"
read n
k=0
p=0
while [ $m -le $n ]
do
((t=m%2))
if [ $t -eq 0 ]
then
((p=p+m))
else
((k=k+m))
fi
((m=m+1))
done
echo "The sum of odd numbers are $k"
echo "The sum of even numbers are $p"
```

Output

```
                    robertkaramagi@robertkaramagi ~/lab
File  Edit  View  Search  Terminal  Help
robertkaramagi@robertkaramagi ~ $ cd lab
robertkaramagi@robertkaramagi ~/lab $ chmod +x ex12.sh
robertkaramagi@robertkaramagi ~/lab $ ls -l ex12.sh
-rwxr-xr-x 1 robertkaramagi robertkaramagi 304 Jan  6 20:27 ex12.sh
robertkaramagi@robertkaramagi ~/lab $ ./ex12.sh
Enter the value of m
1
Enter the value of n
10
The sum of odd numbers are 25
The sum of even numbers are 30
robertkaramagi@robertkaramagi ~/lab $
```

#Find out the max and min number of a given series

ex13.sh.

```
#!bin/bash

echo "Enter the number of elements in the array:"
read n
echo "Enter the elements one by one:"
i=0
while [ $i -lt $n ]
do
read array[$i]
let i++
done
len=${#array[*]}
echo "The array has $len members. They are: "
i=0
while [ $i -lt $len ]
do
echo "$i:${array[$i]}"
let i++
done
i=0
j=1
min=${array[$i]}
max=${array[$i]}
while [ $j -lt $len ]
do
sec=${array[$j]}
if [ $min -gt $sec ]
then
min=$sec
elif [ $max -lt $sec ]
then
max=$sec
fi
let j++
done
echo "Minimum=$min"
echo "Maximum=$max"
```

Output

```
                    robertkaramagi@robertkaramagi ~/lab            _ + x
File  Edit  View  Search  Terminal  Help
robertkaramagi@robertkaramagi ~ $ cd lab
robertkaramagi@robertkaramagi ~/lab $ chmod +x ex13.sh
robertkaramagi@robertkaramagi ~/lab $ ls -l ex13.sh
-rwxr-xr-x 1 robertkaramagi robertkaramagi 614 Jan  6 23:28 ex13.sh
robertkaramagi@robertkaramagi ~/lab $ bash ex13.sh
Enter the number of elements in the array:
6
Enter the elements one by one:
4
78
3
56
789
45
The array has 6 members. They are:
0:4
1:78
2:3
3:56
4:789
5:45
Minimum=3
Maximum=789
robertkaramagi@robertkaramagi ~/lab $ []
```

Implementation of Calculator application

ex14.sh

#!bin/bash

j=1
while [$j -eq 1]
do

echo "Enter the first operand:"
read f1

echo "Enter the second operand:"
read f2

echo "1-> Addition"
echo "2-> Subtraction"
echo "3-> Multiplication"
echo "4-> Division"

echo "Enter your choice"

read n
case "$n" in

1)
echo "Addition"
f3=$((f1+f2))
echo "The result is:$f3"
;;
2)
echo "Subtraction"
let "f4=$f1-$f2"
echo "The result is:$f4"
;;

3)
echo "Multiplication"
let "f5=$f1 * $f2"
echo "The result is:$f5"
;;

4)
echo "Division"
let "f6=$f1 / $f2"
echo "The result is:$f6"
;;

esac
echo "Do you want to continue(press:1 otherwise press any other integer to quit)"

read j

done

Output

```
File Edit View Search Terminal Help
robertkaramagi@robertkaramagi ~ $ cd lab
robertkaramagi@robertkaramagi ~/lab $ chmod +x ex14.sh
robertkaramagi@robertkaramagi ~/lab $ bash ex14.sh
Enter the first operand:
23
Enter the second operand:
23
1-> Addition
2-> Subtraction
3-> Multiplication
4-> Division
Enter your choice
1
```

```
Addition
The result is:46
Do you want to continue(press:1 otherwise press any other integer to quit)
1
Enter the first operand:
20
Enter the second operand:
2
1-> Addition
2-> Subtraction
3-> Multiplication
4-> Division
Enter your choice
2
Subtraction
The result is:18
Do you want to continue(press:1 otherwise press any other integer to quit)
1
Enter the first operand:
24
Enter the second operand:
2
1-> Addition
2-> Subtraction
3-> Multiplication
4-> Division
Enter your choice
3
Multiplication
The result is:48
Do you want to continue(press:1 otherwise press any other integer to quit)
1
Enter the first operand:
24
Enter the second operand:
12
1-> Addition
2-> Subtraction
3-> Multiplication
4-> Division
Enter your choice
4
Division
The result is:2
Do you want to continue(press:1 otherwise press any other integer to quit)
0
```